NAVAL SWORDS

Other volumes in this series
RAPIERS by Eric Valentine
FLINTLOCK PISTOLS by F. Wilkinson
JAPANESE ARMOUR by L. J. Anderson
BLUNDERBUSSES by D. R. Baxter
FRENCH ARMY REGIMENTS AND UNIFORMS
by W. A. Thorburn

1. *Late 17th-century Scallop Shell Hilted Hanger (see pages 22–3)*

NAVAL SWORDS

British and American Naval Edged Weapons
1660–1815

by

P. G. W. ANNIS

ARMS AND ARMOUR PRESS

75014

Published by
Arms and Armour Press
Lionel Leventhal Limited
677 Finchley Road
Childs Hill
London N.W.2.

First published 1970
© P. G. W. Annis, 1970
© Lionel Leventhal Limited, 1970
All rights reserved

85368   046   9

Printed by offset in Great Britain by
William Clowes and Sons Ltd
London and Beccles

Contents

INTRODUCTION

I owe a particular debt of gratitude to the Trustees, Director and Staff of the National Maritime Museum for their encouragement and assistance. I wish to single out Mr. E. H. H. Archibald, of the Department of Pictures, on whose unpublished *Preliminary Descriptive Catalogue of Portraits in Oils* (1961) I have drawn extensively when dealing with photographic reproductions of paintings in the Museum's collection. Commander W. E. May, formerly Deputy Director of the Museum, has always been most generous with his assistance.

I am also indebted for many kindnesses to Mr. Harold L. Peterson who has provided assistance on many occasions and to whose advice I owe much; Mr. William Reid has always been of unfailing help and I am grateful to him also, and I am glad to acknowledge the assistance of Mr. J. P. Puype who has always been prepared to place his profound knowledge of the history of naval dirks at my disposal.

In addition, I wish to thank Captain G. B. K. Griffiths, Royal Marines (Ret.) and Mr. R. L. Kelly for their permission to reproduce photographs of swords in their possession. All photographs used in this study were taken by the photographers of the National Maritime Museum. The great majority of illustrations in this study are of exhibits in that Museum, and to aid their location, Catalogue Numbers have been included in the relevant captions and the abbreviation N.M.M., standing for National Maritime Museum, has been employed throughout. Where the letters G.H. appear the picture concerned forms part of the Greenwich Hospital Collection. The sketches on pages 18–20 are by Mr. D. G. Cufflin.

In spite of this wealth of assistance, I must stress that all opinions and any mistakes are the sole responsibility of the author.

P. G. W. ANNIS

2. *Portrait of Admiral Duncan, 1798, shown wearing a bead-hilted sword (see page 39)*

Naval Swords

Certain criteria need to be established at the outset of this study. The period chosen covers those years in which the Royal Navy grew gradually in size until it became the largest in the world. The fighting navy of the United States of America existed for roughly speaking only the last third of this period while its growth lay well in the future; however, American seamen served in warships and merchant ships throughout this time and many were employed in the British navy. Of these, a proportion were officers and it should be realized that distinctions between specifically British and American naval edged weapons are frequently either difficult to make or insignificant. What are shown here, therefore, are examples of weapon types which are most likely to have been used by both British and American seamen for much of the eighteenth century. More distinctive American styles follow at the end of the period and some attention has been paid to the French origins of some American swords in the late eighteenth and early nineteenth centuries. This brief study has, therefore, been prepared largely from a British point of view and the main emphasis is on the British navy, but it should be remembered that the crews of merchant ships also carried side-arms, and it is never easy to distinguish these from the more common naval weapons.

The period chosen, from 1660 to 1815, covers the appearance of a formal naval organization and growth in Britain, the extension of maritime traditions in America, the continuation and severance of political links between the two countries and, more importantly in the present context, the establishment of recognizable types of edged weapon for seamen. This happened first in Britain, and then in America, a degree of uniformity beginning to appear in both countries towards the end of our period which led eventually to the introduction of regulation patterns. These dates are, of course, only approximate, but they define our concern quite satisfactorily.

The formal organization of the British navy may be said to date from the Restoration: the reforms of the reigns of Charles II and James II gradually produced a spirit of professionalism and an *esprit de corps* which was to be the making of the service and which was to become apparent in America in due course.

Although naval uniform did not make its appearance until the middle of our period, half a century behind France and Spain, the professionalism of seamen had produced by then a measure of uniformity of dress and equipment which stemmed from their calling. This uniformity, approximate though it was, must have appeared more or less simultaneously on both sides of the Atlantic and it had its basic origins in the period of the Restoration.

The eighteenth century, with its wars and revolutions, gave tremendous stimulus to the development of naval weapons and although the British army achieved faster uniformity of dress and personal side-arms at an earlier date than the navy, certain parallel developments took place in the navy and were reflected in America. The success of the 1789 Revolution saw, inevitably, a marked move towards French styles. This move is still demonstrable today if one thinks, for example, of the regulation sword of officers of the United States Navy, but it did not lead to the complete abolition of British styles. It is with this continuing British influence that we are mainly concerned here.

The uniformity of naval dress which began in a formal way in Britain in the middle of the eighteenth century and in America less than half a century afterwards led eventually to regulation pattern swords; these began to appear during the early years of the nineteenth century and, as a period of relative peace was to follow for both countries after the final defeat of Napoleon—a period in which uniformity would be paid more attention than ever before— the date of that defeat forms a convenient point at which to terminate this account. The individuality of British and American naval officers, in their personal choice of weapons within the formal framework of a disciplined service, largely came to an end.

Although blades had to be of iron or steel, and although iron mounts were the cheapest available, this metal does not stand up well to salt-laden air. The more expensive brass was used for mounts, therefore, although when both countries began to arm their ratings, at the end of the eighteenth century, iron mounts, protected by black paint, were adopted, presumably from considerations of cost.

Another general point that may be made is that the deck of a ship was about the last place where one could display swordsmanship and although many eighteenth-century gentlemen, including naval officers, wore small-swords and often had more than an inkling of how to use them, it is unlikely that they were used much at sea on other than occasions of ceremony. Small-swords could be found at sea (in the Spanish navy, for example, where they were regulation wear) but they were hardly the most suitable weapon available. What did appear was the hanger, a weapon long established on shore.

This became almost the badge of the professional seaman and a rather more ornate version was widely worn by officers. In Britain and America it tended to give way, about the middle of the century, to rather longer weapons where officers were concerned, and these in turn were followed by swords which bore as part of their decoration nautical devices emphasizing the calling of their owners. It was this last group which formed the foundation on which regulation patterns were established.

There were further points of similarity between Britain and America: although both had bladesmiths to call upon and the timber, coal and iron necessary for blade production, both imported the great majority of their blades from Germany. Neither country could compete with the volume of production or the cheapness of such centres as Solingen. Yet although Germany could, and did, supply finished weapons, the subsidiary trades connected with turning a blade into a complete sword—the making of guards, grips and scabbards and so on—were in a more fortunate position than that of the blade makers.

In spite of the growth of independent naval services which were relatively free of Army control (in contrast to France or Russia, for example) Army styles exercised considerable influence over both navies. This was probably due, in both cases, to the greater demand for weapons consequent upon the higher degree of uniformity found in land forces and thus the simple availability of such types. In Britain, things went a stage further because the Army's Board of Ordnance exercised control over the supply of virtually all weapons whether to Army or Navy.

Foreign influence, in weapons as in other fields of design, was also common to both countries. Mention has already been made of French influence in America, but it should be remembered that this was just as marked in Britain if in different ways. This was hardly surprising when one thinks of France's accepted pre-eminence in matters of fashion. Both countries abandoned the small-sword and the use of it as a model for presentation swords at about the same time and almost certainly under the influence of changing fashions in Revolutionary France. Both countries adopted a new type of lightweight sword as a replacement, one with a single large shell, on the obverse of the hilt, which was turned towards the point, though this was far more widely adopted in America than in Britain.

Both British and American Marines followed their respective Armies in weapon matters although they were subject to naval rather than to military control.

11

The short, straight or curved hanger employed at the beginning of our period was usually a cheap weapon and must often have been roughly finished; mounts for those issued to ratings were mostly of iron protected by paint, while scabbards, if they existed, were of leather with iron mounts. The advantages of brass, however, were too obvious to be ignored and the widespread use of this metal in the 1740s and 1750s for mounting British infantry hangers was almost certainly followed at sea. So far as officers were concerned, however, other metals were available. Gilt brass was certainly used and so was silver, another metal not prone to rapid corrosion, besides being more applicable as a reflection of an officer's status. Ornate hangers, frequently described today as 'hunting swords' since their decoration often includes allusions to the chase, seem to have been widely adopted by officers. They had the same advantage of handiness as did the cheaper hangers over the more orthodox small-sword, although the latter was worn in large numbers to enhance the dress of men with social pretensions. The difficulty which arises today, in this context, is that few examples of the cheaper type of hanger still exist. From pictorial sources, however, we know that most were simply constructed, often having no guard, but there are others which exhibit a feature of design which, coincidentally, has a pronounced maritime flavour. The scallop shell guard, long in use on land in the seventeenth century, seems to have appeared before 1700 as a variety of hilt for maritime hangers. The large, curved shell provided an effective guard for the hand and the style continued well into the eighteenth century and was widely used in north and north-west Europe. These swords seem often to have had slightly curved blades, but straight examples continued to be used in large numbers, and both Britain and America based their cutlasses on straight patterns though new hilt styles were adopted.

The 'hunting sword', or its derivatives, continued in much the same way as the hanger. The distinctively French form of longer hunting sword, with its slightly curved, single-edged blade and grip which tapered from pommel to guard, became popular on both sides of the Atlantic and remained so until the end of the century (see page 29). In America it seems that it was even more popular than in Britain and, indeed, George Washington himself possessed such a weapon which is now in the Smithsonian Institution. This whole group is characterized by a usually slender, slightly curved blade which has a single edge, a small, ornate cross-guard, and a grip which tapers from the pommel to the guard. These grips were usually bound with silver or copper ribbon, and were mounted by the addition of a ferrule at one end and a pommel cap at the other, both often being of silver. Pommels in Britain tended to be fairly flat, but American makers on occasion favoured the eagle's head device. Many of these weapons were fitted with an oval cup which, being attached to the guard, fitted over the mouth of the scabbard when the weapon was sheathed, thus helping to preserve the blade from water running into the scabbard. Scabbards were of leather and fitted with two or occasionally three metal mounts decorated *en suite* with the guard.

These rather larger 'hunting swords' remained popular when the previous type began to go out of favour and make way for bigger swords exhibiting features already popular with Army officers. Straight infantry swords were worn at sea and so were cavalry swords many of which were curved. Cavalry swords have exercised considerable influence over naval weapons in many countries and neither Britain nor American has been an exception. The stirrup hilt, popular in British naval circles from the late 1790s, was taken from a cavalry original, together with the slightly curved blade with its single broad fuller. This development took place in the last quarter of the eighteenth century and it is interesting to note that a similar development took place in France at about the same time. As a result, some American naval officers wore swords which originally derived from both British and French cavalry patterns.

Another example of the adoption of military styles at sea is furnished by the variant forms of back- and broadsword found in British vessels from the middle of the eighteenth century. These weapons with their usually straight blades and one or two cutting edges were fitted on land with basket hilts. These hilts were possibly less developed at sea but the Scottish broadsword which had a particularly full form of basket was far from being unknown at sea. Interestingly enough, both Britain and America were to adopt basket-hilted swords as regulation patterns later in the nineteenth century.

The seaman's calling, however, was something to be proud of, and it was in the second half of the eighteenth century that the decoration, first of hilts, then of blades, began to reflect this. The most popular device for any seamen was the anchor, the form adopted in Britain being for some unexplained reason the foul anchor (one which has become enmeshed or fouled by its cable). By the time this device became official it was referred to quite simply as 'anchor and cable' in dress regulations, but to most seamen it was, and has remained, 'foul'. Anchors, foul or not, are frequently met with on hilts and blades and some countries adopted the device, either engraved or stamped, as a sign of government ownership. The other common device, generally on better-quality blades, was a representation of a ship or part of a ship—usually a mast with sails and pendants—and the use of 'rope' also became popular, becoming even more so as the nineteenth century wore on.

The use of anchor devices on hilts began in a major way in Britain shortly before the American Revolution and many examples are known where the stirrup-shaped guard is pierced to admit a fretted or openwork foul anchor. The beaded hilt spadroon of the 1780s, which was popular with naval officers into the following century, had often both an openwork anchor within its side-ring and also emulated its military forbear, the infantry sword which became popular in the mid 1780s, by having a metal band round the centre of its grip. Instead of this band bearing some regimental device, a foul anchor surmounted by a crown was engraved there instead. This motif was not to be used formally by the Navy until the dress regulations of 1812 ordered it as a button device, but by that time it was well established and it is probable that its appearance on swords in the late 1780s or early 1790s was the first occasion on which it occurred in a significant way.

Major alterations came at the end of the century when a new British sabre was ordered for light cavalry in 1796. This was soon copied by naval officers and became the pattern for the first regulation naval sword in August 1805 with the addition of a lion's head pommel. This traditional feature, which had appeared on some naval weapons a century or more earlier, was probably taken from the Grenadier and Light Company officer's sword ordered for the Army in 1803. The lion's head was in no way specifically British but was a device which was not only long established but quite international in its scope. Its appearance from relatively early times on American-made hilts is thus hardly surprising.

The hanger had continued into the late eighteenth century primarily, though never exclusively, as a weapon for ratings. It also was becoming more uniform and at the end of the century the British Admiralty began to place orders for batches of such weapons, of a more or less accepted style, to arm ships' companies. A number of makers were involved and it is not certain that a single design was adhered to. Nevertheless, straight, short weapons with black painted iron mounts appeared at this time: the cutlass had come into its own. Similar weapons appeared soon afterwards in America, the Starr Contract of 1799 being a case in point, and only minor changes were made in Britain when the first official pattern appeared in 1804. This pattern was to continue into the 1840s although in both countries experiments were carried out from time to time to see what improvements were necessary.

Having looked briefly at naval swords and cutlasses, we must pay some attention to a third group, the naval dirk. Dirks were worn in both countries, in Britain from about the time of the beginning of the American Revolution, or slightly earlier, and in America from probably rather later. These weapons were unofficial, as were all weapons at first, but both navies took notice of them early in the nineteenth century and ordered restrictions on their use. Nevertheless they were worn by many officers and midshipmen, and, again, it is far from easy to differentiate between British and American specimens except for the fact that British ones are far more common and often slightly more ornate. Why they were worn is a question yet to be answered. It seems that, to a considerable extent, the British navy regarded the dirk as a fighting weapon and it is probable that the same was true of the American. Yet other countries thought of the dirk as a symbol of officer status more convenient in form than the sword. The dirk has come, in more recent years, to be associated almost exclusively with midshipmen, but this is a nineteenth-century development and not true of our period.

Finally, some attention should be paid to presentation weapons. The giving of swords as marks of esteem or as rewards is a practice virtually as old as the weapon itself. Both Britain and America, at the end of the eighteenth century and in the early years of the nineteenth, paid considerable attention to this type of gift, corporate bodies and individuals providing a fair number to officers who distinguished themselves in action or (less often) to those who, over a period of time, rendered consistently valuable service. Cities—especially the City of London—made a number of presentations of small-swords, and so, more interestingly, did the Assemblies of various West Indian islands where politically powerful merchants were most interested in the trade protection provided by the Navy. Similar presentations were also made by the Honourable East India Company. A change in style, away from the small-sword, occurred round about 1800 almost certainly under the influence of Revolutionary France. Although the City of London adhered to the small-sword, at least in some cases, most other organizations followed French practice and chose something else. Patriotic societies also made their mark in this field, on both sides of the Atlantic. Perhaps the best known of these was the Patriotic Fund established at Lloyd's in London. This group of merchants and underwriters resolved on 20 July 1803 that it would be expedient to raise a suitable fund to 'animate the efforts of our defenders by land and sea' and to alleviate the distress of widows, orphans and wounded. In awarding a sword this committee voted a sum of money to the future recipient who then arranged for the production of the weapon. Four main types were produced and these were graded in accordance with the rank or status of the recipient. Midshipmen, Master's Mates and Lieutenants of Royal Marines were awarded weapons of £30 value, Naval Lieutenants and Captains of Royal Marines received £50 swords and Commanders and Captains weapons worth £100. A variant of the £100 sword was awarded to those officers, regardless of rank, who commanded ships at Trafalgar in October 1805. The total number issued was as follows:

Trafalgar pattern: 29
£100 pattern: 39
£50 pattern: 90
£30 pattern: 18

This totals 176 swords; none was awarded to a flag officer and very few went to the Army but both the Royal Marines and the Honourable East India Company were well represented.

Sword-knots

As some misunderstanding has occurred in the past about the significance of the wearing of sword-knots it may be useful to deal with the question here. If we confine ourselves to purely naval considerations, the following picture emerges.

The practice of fitting a length of cord or leather thong to a sword-hilt became popular at sea at the end of the seventeenth century. The loop of cord or leather was attached more or less permanently to the guard near the pommel or to the pommel itself and was wound round the wrist of the user when the sword was drawn in order that the weapon should not be lost even if struck from his hand. As the eighteenth century wore on the more ornate swords came to be decorated with either a length of woven silk tape or a cord of twisted silk. From about 1750 these attachments tended to be coloured blue and yellow, presumably in imitation of the recently introduced uniform for naval officers. Rather later the yellow silk gradually came to be replaced by gilt wire, possibly round about the time that epaulettes were introduced, of the type already employed for weaving rank-distinction lace. There were no regulations covering these knots which, incidentally, had probably long ceased to be regarded as anything other than decorative features. (This is hardly surprising when one remembers that there were no regulations covering the swords themselves.)

16

Sword-knots were found on both civil and military swords. Small-swords, which were worn by many officers in full dress, were frequently decorated by blue and gold silk knots and although civilians often wore such attachments, in a variety of colours, it is possible, if no more, that this was done to give a service appearance to an essentially civilian weapon. The tape form was the most popular and was usually arranged wrapped round the guard in such a way as to hide nearly all of it. Round about 1790 a development of this type appeared. To the flat terminal tassel was added an embroidered foul anchor just as two decades earlier this same device had begun to make its appearance on sword-hilts. The introduction of presentation swords, particularly those of the Patriotic Fund, led to a requirement for a more decorative knot; swords awarded by the Fund were fitted with a blue and gold cord to the end of which was attached a large gold barrel-shaped mould from which depended gold bullions. This heavier and more distinctive type was probably imitated by a number of officers for their rather less ornate personal weapons following the demise of the small-sword on which it would have appeared both clumsy and ungraceful.

From this was but a short step to the beginnings of the sword-knot as we know it today and uniform patterns appeared in Britain in the 1820s, being enforced by regulations from 1827.

Dirks were treated quite differently in Britain. Knots for these small weapons were probably very uncommon in the late eighteenth and early nineteenth centuries and, indeed, only became regulation wear in the second half of the nineteenth century.

The practice in America seems to have been very similar to that outlined above though there may be grounds for thinking that, at first, the sword-knot was rather less common than in Britain. Regulation forms appeared in the nineteenth century and blue and gold were the colours adopted.

What can also be said of both countries is that the sword-knot did not achieve anything like the status it possessed in continental Europe. Although, from time to time, different patterns were ordered for different ranks, no great importance seems to have been attached to this. A sword or dirk without a knot, in either Britain or America, might offend against the regulations and might even result in the officer concerned being ordered to buy one. In Germany, on the other hand, the absence of a dirk knot was as precise a mark of rank as its presence; what had begun as a decorative feature, a part of the long-established practice of decorating a personal weapon, became in time something to be earned.

17

Nomenclature

As there is no agreed international system for naming the parts of the sword many different terms have come into use and this has, occasionally, led to some confusion. The terms used here are those employed by the author and there is no pretence that they are in any way preferable to different terms adopted by others. Generally speaking, the terms used are those based on British naval dress regulations but where these are not appropriate recourse has been made to the writings of others and to the comments of friends. What is important about any term is that it should have, if not the sanction of regulations, at least a logical and descriptive basis. A fair number

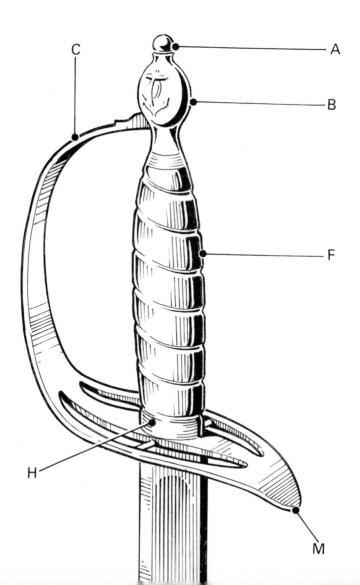

of alternative terms exist, but the meaning of those used here may be illustrated by the following sketches showing the principal terms associated here with sword-hilts.

A Tang button: a metal fitting over which the end of the tang is burred; occasionally, on good-quality swords, this fitting is threaded internally and screws onto the end of the tang.
B Pommel: strictly a knob which locates the end of the guard and grip; used here, on occasion, to describe the end of a hilt when it forms a part of a back-piece (G).
C Knuckle-guard: the meaning is self-evident, but when a more or less smooth curve is followed from top to bottom of the hilt the term *knuckle-bow* has been employed instead.

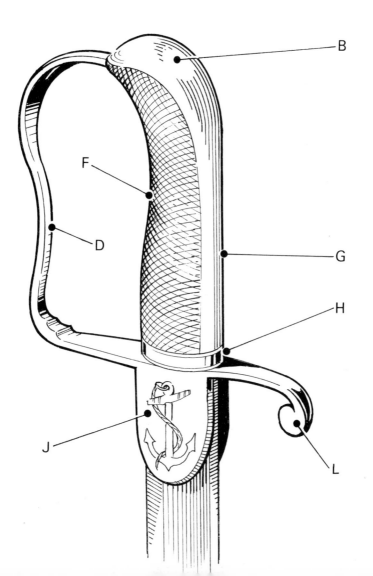

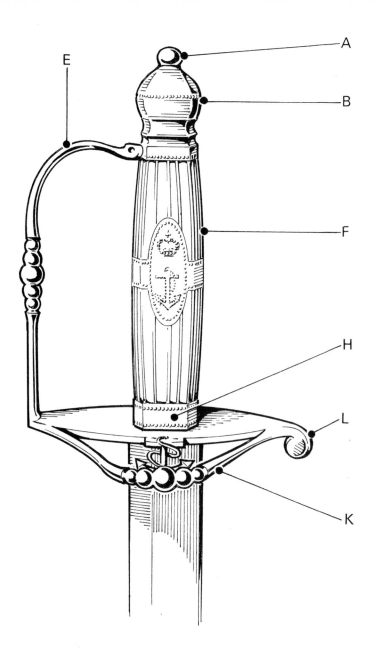

D Stirrup guard: this form has a convex curve from the pommel followed by a concave one to a sharp angle at the forward end of the horizontal cross-guard, it is often referred to as a 'reverse P shape'.

E Straight stirrup guard: this pattern, which is found chronologically before and after D, curves from the pommel and meets the cross-guard at a right angle.

F Grip: the meaning is again self-evident, but if the outline is curved to be wider near the blade than it is at the pommel, it is referred to as shaped to the hand.

G Back-piece: this is usually made in one piece with the type of pommel shown in sketch 3 and serves to strengthen the grip.

H Ferrule: this locates and reinforces the end of the grip in the same way as the pommel.

J Langet: an oval or shield-shaped extension to the cross-guard projecting over the shoulder of the blade: it is, perhaps, a descendant of the ancient 'waterguard' designed to protect the blade when it is sheathed.

K Side-ring: a self-contained addition to the cross-guard lying in the same horizontal plane. Almost always found in the eighteenth century on the obverse side only, it can take a variety of shapes and may have some device placed within it.

L Quillon: the arm of the cross-guard, usually found at the rear though on many swords an additional arm appears at the front.

M Stool: the more or less horizontal plate of the guard between grip and blade which extends to the rear and replaces the quillon, the narrow section of which would be inappropriate on so wide a guard.

Most blade terms are self-explanatory but, where a single-edged blade has a part of its back sharpened near the point and leading to it this additional feature is referred to here as a *false edge*. Many blades are unsharpened for a brief space where they join the guard; this part is referred to here as the *shoulder* of the blade. Any groove cut longitudinally into the surface of a blade is referred to as a *fuller*. Blades lacking any such feature and also lacking a ridge behind the cutting edge are referred to as *flat*. If the greatest width of a blade is found at a position a few inches short of the point then the type is generally referred to as a *falchion* or *falchion-shaped*; such blades are always curved.

Scabbards are fitted with metal mounts to which means of suspension are attached. These mounts are here called *lockets*. Suspension may be by a ring or rings or by a stud fitted near the top of the scabbard known as a *frog-hook* or *frog-stud*. The tip of a scabbard is often protected not only by a mount known as a *chape* but that feature is itself often protected by a strip of metal called a *shoe*. This last feature can take a variety of forms.

21

3, 4. *Scallop Shell Hilted Hanger, late 17th century* (see also Plate 1)

This weapon has a horn grip and iron hilt mounts. These consist of two scallop-shaped pieces either side of the grip which are curved towards the pommel and decorated on their outer faces to simulate sea-shells. A forward extension, also curved towards the pommel, has a small 'shell' at its tip and acts as a knuckle-guard. An iron cap is placed over the end of the grip to provide an anchorage for the end of the tang thus doing service as a pommel. A small tang button is placed in the centre of this but this feature is a modern replacement. Within the guard, slots are cut in the iron sheet in a way which was to become very popular a century later. The blade is single-edged, flat-backed and slightly curved. Two fullers run nearly the whole length and a narrower one appears against the back, terminating at the start of the false edge which is pronounced. In each of the two principal fullers there is cut the word VALENC. This is presumably a reference to the Spanish town of Valencia, but it is likely that the blade is German in origin. The hilt is quite possibly English. This style of weapon was very widespread right across northern and western Europe in the seventeenth and early eighteenth centuries. Although the use of a maritime motif for the guard does not necessarily indicate that the weapon was intended for sea-service, since many obviously cavalry weapons have similar features, this type of weapon, with its short, heavy, curved blade was widely associated with the sea. In the public mind, there is even a particular association with pirates, but there can be little doubt that, to a great extent, this type represents the beginnings of that group of more or less specialized weapons connected with seamen of all sorts which reached its scientific apotheosis in the cutlass. It was an ancestor of the

22

hangers of the eighteenth century and it may not be too fanciful to see the beginnings of the late eighteenth-century hilt form in this type. This particular weapon has a knuckle-guard which does not reach the pommel but many others had longer guards which did, and which were secured at the end by a screw to the pommel itself. No particular nationality can really be attributed to the style shown here. There are similar weapons in Denmark and the Netherlands which are probably native to those countries. There are also, in the same places, rather simpler weapons of roughly the same date. Some of these have no guards, others have a single scallop shell acting as a knuckle-guard. Nearly all have bone or horn grips and short, heavy, curved blades. John Esquemeling's book, *Bucaniers of America* (London, 1684), illustrates a number of swords of this type in some of the portraits it contains.

Blade: 24·3"   Hilt: 5·4"   N.M.M. 430

5. *Hunting Sword, c. 1700*

Reference was made in the introduction to the widespread use of 'hunting swords' at sea and this example is quite typical of the plainer type used. It has a staghorn grip and brass hilt. The knuckle-bow form of guard divides opposite the ferrule and a bar sweeps to the rear on the obverse side of the cross having, in one piece with it, a roughly oval shell which fills the space between that bar and the remainder of the guard itself. There is a short quillon with a lobated finial. The blade is flat-backed and single-edged and has a small false edge. It is flat and bears a mark in the form of a king's head on each side. This mark has not been identified but it is almost certainly German and it is entirely possible that the whole sword was made in that country. The scabbard is missing but we may assume it was of leather with brass mounts. Decoration has been kept to a minimum and, apart from the grip itself, consists of a single engraved thread on the ferrule and twin threads on the pommel cap. In comparison with some of those weapons shown in the portrait paintings of Dahl and Kneller, this sword is on the plain side and it may be assumed that it is therefore more representative of the types of 'hunting sword' worn at sea.

Blade: 19″ Hilt: 5·25″ N.M.M. 226

6. *Portrait of John Benbow, 1701*

John Benbow (1653–1702) served in the merchant navy and so success-fully established his reputation as a seaman that he was accepted into the Royal Navy as a Captain in 1689. He later achieved flag rank and became Commander-in-Chief in the West Indies. He died of wounds after an action with a French squadron which lasted for six consecutive days. This portrait was painted by Sir Godfrey Kneller in 1701 and shows Benbow in the civilian dress of the time (there being no uniform then) over which he wears a breastplate. Whether even this limited amount of armour was worn much at sea we cannot tell. Back- and breastplates were part of a ship's stores in the sixteenth century but it is likely that they fell into disuse in the seventeenth. The sitter holds, in his right hand, a fairly simple form of hanger which is probably typical of the plainer sort favoured by some officers in the early eighteenth century. The blade is short, curved, single-edged and flat-backed. The hilt is of some yellow metal and is made up of a simple, rather angular knuckle-guard which leads to a short rear quillon and has minimal decoration in the form of three beads at its centre point. It is not easy to distinguish much detail about the pommel save for the fact that it is domed, possibly even globular, and covered with decoration in high relief. The grip is hidden.

N.M.M. G.H. 141

26

7, 8. *Portrait of Clowdisley Shovell, 1702*

Mention was made in the introduction of the gradual change from the short hanger to a longer, heavier sword as the eighteenth century wore on. This change really only becomes apparent in the middle of the century, but, of course, larger swords had never disappeared from sea service and examples of those developed during and after the English Civil War must have been quite well known. This portrait, and the accompanying detail from it, of Sir Clowdisley Shovell, show this quite well. Painted by Michael Dahl in 1702, it portrays the Admiral in armour, not because he made a habit of wearing it but because this practice served to magnify the subject. Shovell's services were such that he must have been a household name. He served in the Mediterranean from 1673 to 1686 and first came to prominence for his work in destroying shipping in Tripoli harbour in 1675. He received his knighthood for his services at Bantry Bay three years after returning from the Mediterranean, played an important part in the defeat of the French at Barfleur in 1692 and assisted in the capture of Gibraltar and the Battle of Malaga in 1704. He next served as Commander-in-Chief in the Mediterranean, leaving for home in 1707. His ship, the *Association*, 96, was wrecked on the Scilly Isles and Shovell only just managed to get ashore. While lying exhausted on the beach he was murdered for his emerald ring by a woman of the island. Just as the use of armour serves to glorify the sitter, the long and fairly ornate sword he is depicted as wearing is a suitable weapon for a fighting man and is sufficiently workmanlike for a seaman. The hilt is yellow in colour and is therefore, presumably, of brass. It seems to have a lion's head pommel though this is apparently in a grotesque form. The knuckle-bow is quite simple and probably leads to both front and rear quillons, only the former of which can be seen. The blade is apparently straight, or nearly so, and probably quite broad. Whether it is single- or double-edged we cannot say, but the general impression is one of weight. Although it cannot be seen very clearly, this sword is obviously larger than any hanger and, trusting to Dahl's reputation for accuracy, may well have been used at sea.

N.M.M.

27

9. *Portrait of Charles Brown, 1740*

Evidence of the continuing popularity of the hanger type of weapon is not difficult to find. This portrait of Commodore Charles Brown (*c.* 1680–1753) was executed by an unknown artist in 1740. It was in the previous year that Brown, as second in command to Vernon in the West Indies, commanded the *Hampton Court*, 70, in operations against Porto Bello, and won fame for his capture of the Iron Castle, the principal defensive work. The Spanish commander of the castle attempted to surrender his own sword to Brown but was referred to Vernon. Vernon then gave that sword, a silver hilted small-sword, to Brown as a memento of the action. Brown is shown in his portrait holding a form of hanger. The hilt is yellow in the picture (presumably the original was of brass) and is made up of a fluted flattened oval pommel, a simple knuckle-guard decorated by a bead at its mid-point and a single (rear) quillon which curls towards the blade. The blade itself is single-edged and apparently flat-backed. There is a slight suggestion of a fuller, or at least some hollowing, for roughly two-thirds of its length, but this is not apparent at the shoulder.
N.M.M. G.H. 169

10. *French Hunting Sword, c. 1765*

A longer, slightly curved form of hunting sword which first appeared in France. The weapon shown here is a good example of this type. It is supposed to have been taken by a British naval officer after the capture of the French frigate *La Cléopatre* by H.M.S. *Nymphe* on 18 June 1793. The polished and spirally grooved wooden grip tapers from the pommel to the ferrule at the other end and is bound with copper ribbon. The hilt mounts are of embossed silver and include vestigial langets which incorporate an inverted cup fitting over the mouth of the scabbard when the weapon is sheathed. The silver mounts are stamped with the mark of a Paris maker. The blade is slightly curved, flat-backed and has a single broad fuller each side. Its engraved decoration is military in character and includes trophies of guns, pikes, flags and drums. The black leather scabbard has two silver mounts which bear partly chased and partly embossed decoration very similar to that found on the hilt. This style of hanger was popular in France, Britain and America. Many were made in both Britain and America. American manufacturers produced quite a number which had chain or even knuckleguards. H. L. Peterson's *American Silver Mounted Swords* (see Bibliography) includes a selection of these.
Blade: 23·5″ Hilt: 6·5″ N.M.M. 266

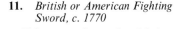

11. *British or American Fighting Sword, c. 1770*

This type of sword, with its two slots cut into the guard on each side of the grip, was widely popular on both sides of the Atlantic. The date given above is only approximate, but there is pictorial evidence (see, for example, plates 14 and 15) to support it. All hilt mounts are of brass, and the urn-shaped pommel may indicate that this sword dates from slightly later than *c.* 1770; it is decorated with an engraved foul anchor, an early example of the use of this device. The grip is of polished dark brown wood into which a spiral groove has been cut for a simulated binding. This binding is now missing but probably consisted of a ribbon of brass or copper. The blade is curved, single-edged and flat-backed, with a single broad fuller running from the shoulder to the point. A number of similar weapons are known on both sides of the Atlantic but as no regulations for them have been found it must be assumed that the style was simply a very popular one. No makers are connected with any of these so it may be further assumed that the majority of blades are German in origin and that hilts were made both in Britain and

America. The style of guard became popular in Britain some years before the outbreak of the American Revolution and it remained so until the end of the century. Very similar weapons, albeit with different blades, are shown in Mr. Peterson's *The American Sword* (Philadelphia, 1965), pages 62 and 66.
Blade: 29·5″   Hilt: 6″   N.M.M. 353

30

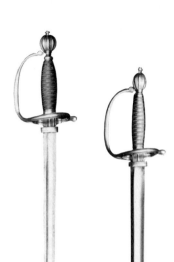

12. *Two Swords with Oval Side-ring Hilts, 1780–90*

These two swords are so similar that it is as well to show them both. There are a number of similar ones in existence and it is evident that the style must have been popular for a considerable period. In spite of varying dimensions, one description will serve for both, as the only obvious difference in general appearance lies in the fact that No. 61 has a hilt mounted with silver gilt and the other has one of gilt brass. Both have simple knuckle-bows, ribbed and fluted oval pommels, a vestigial ricasso and an oval loop of metal attached to the obverse side of the guard between knuckle-bow and quillon. No. 61 bears the marks for London in 1785/6 together with the maker's mark I.F., which may stand for John Fayle, but this by no means certain. The other sword may be slightly older. Lord Nelson apparently purchased a very similar weapon after 1803 so the continuing popularity of the style is obvious. Cut-and-thrust blades are fitted to both swords and both have black leather scabbards with gilt mounts. An additional point of interest is furnished by the presence of a small cup, oval in shape, fitted to the guard in such a way as to enclose the top of the scabbard when the sword is sheathed. This feature, it will be remembered, was also found on French style 'hunting swords' which were so popular in America in the last quarter of the eighteenth century. This form of fitting was long established when these swords were made but virtually disappeared soon after this date in both Britain and America.

Left—Blade: 29·5″   Hilt: 6″
N.M.M. 61
Right—Blade: 31·25″   Hilt: 6·25″
N.M.M. 304

31

13, 14. *British Fighting Sword, c. 1782*

This sword is worthy of treatment at some length because it demonstrates both the continuing popularity of the slotted guard for the hilt, already noted, and the firm establishment in Britain of the practice of using maritime motifs for decorative purposes—a practice which has continued to the present day. It also demonstrates the continuing use of the stirrup form of guard, something unknown with small-swords, and the use of multiple wire binding of the grip which by this date was beginning to disappear from fighting weapons. These two photographs between them show all these features. The stirrup guard is pierced at the front by a trapezium-shaped hole and has additional piercings each side of the cross-guard, the reverse slot being bridged by a short bar. On the obverse and at the front, a fretted foul anchor supplies the decoration and indicates very clearly the calling of the wearer. Though never a regulation pattern, this style of hilt was very popular. The pommel of the example illustrated here is flat but others are known which are domed and fluted. All hilt mounts are of gilt brass. The grip is bound with fine copper wire over which is superimposed twin strands of thicker silver wire arranged spirally at intervals. The blade is straight, single-edged and flat-backed, being relatively thick in section. It has a false edge

some 9 inches long and a single broad fuller running the whole length. Its engraved decoration is minimal consisting only of the Royal coat of arms with the motto DIEU ET MON DROIT on both sides. The scabbard is of black leather and fitted with two gilt brass lockets, each with a ring, and a gilt brass chape. What is probably the original sword-knot is still attached and consists of a ribbon of blue and yellow silk with a blue and yellow silk tassel attached to the end. Although this sword is not particularly large it is relatively heavy. Its comparatively short blade which has the advantage of handiness has been deliberately strengthened and made more suitable for fighting by increasing its thickness. The scabbard mounts, on the other hand, as they would rarely come under any great strain, unlike those of an army sword, are quite light. This sword was supplied by Cullum of Charing Cross, London, his name appearing on the reverse of the top locket, to Sir Samuel Hood (1762–1814).

Blade: 29·25″ Hilt: 5·5″ N.M.M. 305

15. *Detail of a portrait of Charles Saunders, 1772/3*

Sir Charles Saunders (1713?–75) was one of the officers who accompanied George Anson on part of his voyage of circumnavigation in 1740–4, as a Lieutenant in the *Centurion*, 64. He later served in a variety of capacities and became famous for his services at Quebec in 1759 where, as a Vice-Admiral, he commanded the fleet which conveyed and supported Wolfe's army. This portrait, by Richard Brompton (1734–82), shows Saunders in the full dress uniform of a flag officer of the period 1767–83. In his right hand the sitter holds an example of the slotted hilt form of sword which was, as we have seen, so popular in the 1770s. The wire-bound grip and the slightly curved stool are clearly visible. Round the guard is wrapped a blue and gold sword-knot of the tape variety which was more popular than the cord where relatively light-weight hilts were concerned. This and other pictures demonstrate that knots of this type were frequently worn wrapped round the guard at this time rather than knotted as was the later fashion. N.M.M. G.H. 63

16. *British Fighting Sword, c. 1775*

This weapon probably originated as a normal form of slotted hilt type. Round about the end of the eighteenth century an additional bar was added to the obverse, incorporating a crown and anchor badge, to fill the space between it and the existing guard. This is just one piece of evidence for suggesting that the knuckle-bow form of guard, together with its variant forms, was regarded by some as offering inadequate protection to the hand. The cutlass which appeared at about this time had a large guard and the first proper regulation sword, the wearing of which was enforced (that of 1827), bore a half-basket in place of the narrow stirrup which preceded it. The guard of this weapon is of brass and the grip of vertically fluted wood. There is some suggestion that the Honourable East India Company preferred black or dark brown grips round about 1800 though the crown and anchor badge here makes it clear that the Company was not concerned with this weapon. The blade is relatively short, curved, single-edged and flat-backed. It has two fullers, a narrow one near the back and a more central broad shallow one. The whole weapon, in short, may be regarded as a development of the hanger form as well as an example of the slotted hilt type in a British context. This latter point is of interest because there is evidence to suggest that the type continued to be popular in the United States for rather longer than in Britain. Mr. Peterson gives an example of this in *The American Sword* (No. 95).

Blade: 24·75″   Hilt: 4·4″   N.M.M. 306

17. *Portrait of Richard Kempenfelt, 1781–2*

This portrait of Rear-Admiral Kempenfelt (1718–82) shows quite clearly one of the popular forms of fighting sword used in the Royal Navy in the early 1780s. Painted by Tilly Kettle (1735–86) shortly before the sitter died when his flagship the *Royal George*, 100, was lost at Spithead in August 1782, this portrait demonstrates the continuing popularity of the hanger type of weapon. The hilt is apparently of gilt brass and of the straight stirrup form. Although the artist does not make it very clear, it is almost certain that the guard is in fact of the slotted type. The grip is apparently bound with wire and metal ribbon and the pommel is globular in shape, surmounted by a fairly prominent tang button. The blade, though hidden by its scabbard, is obviously curved and fairly broad and is also rather longer than those hanger blades met earlier in the eighteenth century. The scabbard is black, fitted with the usual three gilt mounts, and suspended by its rings from two slings worn under the Admiral's coat. The top locket of this scabbard appears to be relatively small but it was the custom of the time, in many countries, to make this part longer on the obverse than the reverse. What is also of interest here is the demonstration that flag-officers wore fighting swords of this essentially simple type for much the same reason as their juniors. Kempenfelt is shown in undress uniform so it could be that this fighting sword was regarded as more appropriate than the more conventional small-sword.
N.M.M. G.H. 99

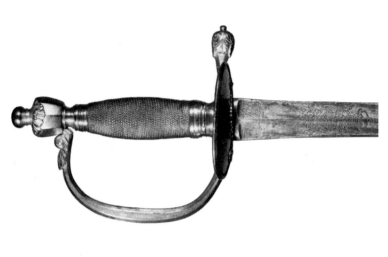

18. *British Infantry Officer's Sword, 1797*

This sword is an example of that formally introduced for British infantry officers on 4 May 1796.* It is of a style which was probably known before that year and can be dated 1797 by reference to the maker's style of name and address: PROSSER, LATE CULLUM . . . CHARING CROSS (London). John Prosser took over from James Cullum in 1797 and for about a year used the words 'late Cullum' after his own name. It is apparent that British Marine officers adopted this pattern of sword at about the same time as the Army and it is included here because it was often found at sea. It is of further interest in that it provided the model on which some United States Engineer officer's swords of the early nineteenth century were based. It furnishes a British example of a whole range of European swords which probably originated in the Prussian infantry sword of the 1740s. The widespread use of acanthus decoration, the general shape of the pommel and the obvious derivation from the small-sword form are all worthy of note. The hilt consists of a gilt brass pommel decorated with acanthus leaves, silver wire wound grip, gilt knuckle-bow to a quillon with acanthus decoration at its finial and twin gilt shells. These are both fixed but on many examples the reverse shell will fold flat against the top locket when the sword is sheathed. The blade is straight and of a flattened diamond section. Most swords of this pattern had straight cut-and-thrust blades with a single edge and short false edge. The black leather scabbard has the usual three gilt mounts and both a frog stud and suspension rings. A final point of interest about this weapon concerns the blade which has a small longitudinal flat engraved with the words FOR MY COUNTRY AND KING. A fair number of blades bearing this motto appeared at the end of the eighteenth century and they seem to have enjoyed a vogue for some years.

Blade: 32·5″   Hilt: 6″   N.M.M. 102

* Public Record Office, W.O. 3/28, p. 165.

19. *British Bead-Hilt Spadroon, 1790–1805*

It is probable that this pattern of sword first appeared in the British Army in the mid 1780s. It is often, though incorrectly, referred to as the infantry officer's sword of 1786 although it was, presumably, known rather earlier. The hilt has a straight stirrup form of guard with a side-ring on the obverse at the cross. Both the stirrup and the side-ring are decorated with five beads which led to the popular description of this type as the 5-ball sword. Army regulations provided for hilts to be the same colour as uniform buttons. Those regiments which had gilt buttons had gilt sword-hilts and those which had silver buttons mounted their swords with silver or, more commonly, steel. Round about 1790, naval officers adopted the same form of sword with gilt brass mounts. They retained the Army practice of fitting the grip with a metal band, but in place of a regimental cypher or badge adopted the unofficial device of a crown over a foul anchor. This device did not become official until it was ordered for uniform buttons in 1812, but by that time it was a long-established and popular feature. Some examples of this sword had urn-shaped pommels but the type shown here, the cushion pommel, became far better known. The grip, as was often the case, is of vertically reeded ivory. The blade is of the spadroon, or cut-and-thrust, type. This type was frequently ordered in both Britain and America and can never have been truly successful at either of its functions. A cutting blade needs to be curved and of elongated section and a thrusting blade ought to be straight, stiff and of compact section. It is single-edged, flat-backed with a short false edge and has a broad, shallow fuller each side. This style of sword became widely popular and was known in countries as far apart as Norway and Denmark in the

North, Bavaria in the South and America in the West. In France it was known as the *épée Anglais* and it probably lasted longer in the United States than in any other country, the Infantry officer's sword of 1821 being a case in point.

Blade: 32″   Hilt: 5·75″   N.M.M. 6

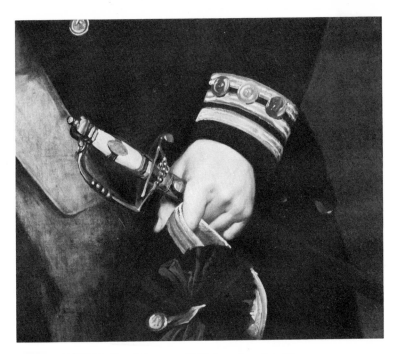

20. *Portrait of Admiral Duncan, 1798 (see also plate 2)*

This portrait of Admiral Viscount Duncan, painted by the American artist John Singleton Copley, shows an example of the widely-used bead-hilted (or 5-ball) sword. Duncan (1731–1804) won the Battle of Camperdown over the Dutch fleet in 1797 and this portrait was painted in the following year. The Admiral is shown wearing the undress uniform of his rank of the pattern in force from 1795 to 1812. His sword has a yellow mounted white grip and has been observed accurately enough to give some idea of its detail. No fretted anchor is to be seen within the side-ring and the gilt band which surrounds the centre of the grip is apparently plain. The cushion pommel and beaded straight stirrup guard and side-ring show clearly. It is possible that the rather less common smooth form of ivory grip is shown. Little can be made of the rest of the sword beyond the assumptions that the blade is straight and that the scabbard is of black leather fitted with gilt mounts. It is likely that Duncan continued to wear this sword for the remainder of his service. He is shown in a number of other pictures wearing either this weapon or one very similar and thus he represents the last of the generation of officers with whom the pattern was so popular.
N.M.M.

21. *Detail of a painting of Lord Howe at the Battle of 1st June, 1794*

This painting was executed by Mather Brown in 1794, shortly after the action it depicts. The subject is primarily Richard, 1st Earl Howe, but of interest to this study are two figures on the extreme right of the picture and these are shown here. The two men concerned are Captain Sir Andrew Snape Douglas (1761–97) and his nephew Midshipman Graham Eden Hamond (1779–1862). Douglas is portrayed holding a bead-hilted spadroon. A further point of interest is the blued and gilt blade of that weapon. There have been suggestions that such decorated blades would never have been used in action, but as the painter of this picture went to considerable trouble to sketch the principals from life and to get other details accurate, it would seem that on occasion they were so used. Hamond is wearing a simple dirk which demonstrates the beginning of the move away from the rather angular weapons of the last quarter of the eighteenth century. It apparently consists of a reeded ivory grip, brass or gilt brass pommel cap decorated with flutes and a short cross-guard which may have both quillons turned towards the point of the blade. This last is apparently straight. Douglas served in the action as Captain of Howe's flagship the *Queen Charlotte*, 100. He was wounded in the head and died of the after-effects of that wound three years later.
N.M.M.

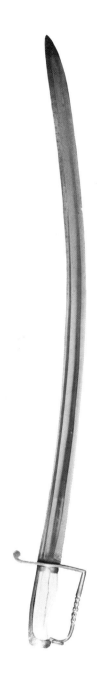

22. *Fighting Sword, c. 1800*

The hilt of this sword offers an example of one of the many variations of the bead or 5-ball type popular in Britain and America from the late eighteenth century until the middle 1820s. Simpler than the classical pattern and lacking any side-ring, this weapon is interesting because it also has a grip which is shaped to the hand instead of being parallel sided, or nearly so, as were earlier weapons of this general type. It was made in Britain, by Harvey of Birmingham, but exhibits no other feature which might carry the story further. The hilt has an ivory grip with gilt brass mounts and the blade is slightly curved, flat-backed and has both a broad fuller and a shorter narrow one at the back edge. This might be con-sidered to be a rather old-fashioned design by the end of the eighteenth century. Similar weapons are known in America and this sword could have been made for the American market but there is no evidence to support this suggestion. This is of a type popular with naval and cavalry officers on both sides of the Atlantic. The combination of a beaded guard with a grip shaped to the hand may be considered to be a relatively late feature.

Blade: 29·24″ Hilt: 4·6″ N.M.M. 297

23. *French Fighting Sword, c. 1800*

This sword is included here because, with many similar weapons, it forms an example of the type of French sword adopted by officers of the United States Navy. Like one of its British contemporaries, this sword owes its origins to a light cavalry pattern. The grip is of ebony decorated with diagonal flutes and mounted with gilt brass. It can be seen that no back-piece is fitted but that the pommel, with its fluted and domed end, is supported by a fairly lengthy extension over the grip. The stirrup-shaped guard incorporates double langets (i.e., langets which extend above and below the cross-piece) and these bear embossed foul anchors. The blade is slightly curved, flat-backed and has a single broad fuller running most of its length. It is lightly engraved each side with designs having classical

military allusions. It will be noticed that, in a way which probably originated in France, the pommel is inclined forward. This feature was to be adopted by many countries, Germany in particular, in the nineteenth century, but examples are also found in America, the naval officer's sword of 1852 being the best known. France exercised an influence over the swords of other countries which, until the second half of the nineteenth century, was probably unequalled.

Blade: 30·25″   Hilt: 5″   N.M.M. 49

24. *British Fighting Sword, c. 1800*

This sword offers a relatively early example of the adoption of a version of the light cavalry sword of 1796 by a British naval officer. The cavalry weapon had iron mounts whereas naval versions were fitted with gilt brass. This style, with its stirrup-shaped guard, was to spread eventually all over Europe and the Americas and was itself, to some extent, a development of earlier and straighter stirrup guards in Britain. The guard incorporates langets which bear an engraved foul anchor. The back-piece forms a single part with the smooth and entirely plain pommel. The grip is of white ivory cross-hatched overall and is secured by the pommel at one end and by a small gilt ferrule at the other. The guard is pierced by a slot near the pommel to take a sword-knot. This knot consists of a double ribbon of blue silk into which have been woven three yellow silk stripes and to which has been added a fringe of gold silk. A woven turk's-head knot, also of silk and acting as a slide, completes this piece. The blade is curved, single-edged and flat-backed with a small false edge. A broad, shallow fuller runs for virtually the whole length each side. There are traces of the original blue and gilt decoration remaining. The black leather scabbard has the usual two gilt brass lockets, each with a ring, and a gilt chape fitted with a small shoe. The top locket has a frog stud in addition to its ring which either indicates that the method of suspension changed or that the stud was to afford additional security when the wearer was engaged in boat service. The suppliers of this weapon were Hill and Yardley of 3, Charing Cross, London.

Blade: 27·9″   Hilt: 5″   N.M.M.

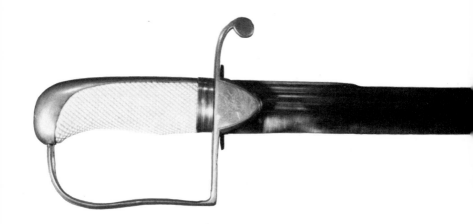

25. *British Fighting Sword, 1800*

This sword, though apparently much the same as that shown previously is worthy of note because of its decoration, albeit limited, and the shape of its blade. The grip is of ivory, cross-hatched overall and the hilt mounts are of gilt brass, the guard being pierced for a sword-knot. The langets, however, instead of bearing the usual engraved foul anchor are engraved with naval trophies. That on the obverse, though very faint, consists of an oval shield bearing the Union Flag superimposed on crossed anchor, cannon, musket, rammer and flag pole with pendant. Although this motif, and many like it, may be found on a number of blades it is rather less often found on hilts. The blade is curved and single-edged with a flat back. It is strengthened at the shoulder by being made a quarter of an inch wider than elsewhere; this is not a common feature for a naval sword produced under the influence of the light cavalry form of 1796, and the addition of two nearly full-length fullers together with a short one coextensive with the addition at the shoulder seems to indicate other influences. It is possible that this blade was taken from another sword and there is a strong suggestion about it which leads to the assumption that it is a good deal older than the hilt. The black leather scabbard has two gilt lockets with rings and a chape. It is covered, on the obverse, with blind tooling of a geometrical pattern such as was old-fashioned by 1800. The top locket of this scabbard, however, bears the supplier's name and address—Tatham, 37 Charing Cross—which dates it almost exactly as Henry Tatham opened at that address in 1800 and the name of the firm changed to Tatham and Egg in 1802. It is probably an example both of continuing individualism and, more important, serious attention being paid to sword-design on the part of an owner.
Blade: 30·5″ Hilt: 4·75″ N.M.M. 1

26. *Detail of a portrait of James Newman-Newman, c. 1801*

Captain Newman joined the Royal Navy shortly after the American War of Independence. He was born in 1767 and lost his life in 1811 on his way home from the Baltic when his ship, the *Hero*, 74, went aground off the Texel in company with two other vessels. This portrait, by A. J. Oliver, was first exhibited in 1801 and it is likely that it was painted that year. Newman is shown in the full-dress uniform of a Captain of over three years in the rank and he holds, in his right hand, an interesting variant form of the sword which had recently become popular in the Navy. Here, the plain stirrup hilted sword has been taken as a model but the result is some distance away from the original. The finial of the quillon is apparently pointed and resembles a four-sided arrow-head. To reflect this, the langets appear as a simple diamond-shape rather longer over the blade than over the hilt. The grip is, as usual, of ivory or some similar material but, apart from limited fluting, is unlike that normally found. The blade is presumably curved and single-edged. A sword-knot of the tape variety is wrapped round the knuckle-guard but it terminates in tassels instead of a flat slide with a fringe. It is, apparently, of gold tape with a narrow blue thread. N.M.M.

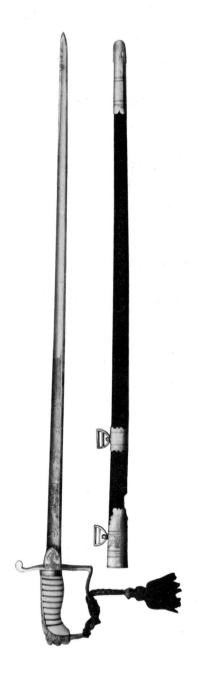

27. British Officer's Sword, 1805

In documents of August 1805* a regulation pattern of sword was mentioned for British naval officers. The regulations were apparently rather vague and large numbers of officers ignored them, but there are sufficient examples about today to indicate that the new sword found favour with many. The stirrup hilt, which had been used by the Navy for some five years, was the pattern chosen but to it was added a lion's mask pommel and, usually, a straight blade of the popular cut-and-thrust type. The sword illustrated here formerly belonged to the Earl of St. Vincent and is illustrated in a portrait of that officer by Pellegrini painted in 1806. The grip is of ivory bound with gilt wire and the hilt mounts are of gilt brass throughout. They consist of a stirrup guard incorporating langets which bear an engraved foul anchor, a lion's mask pommel made in one with a smooth back-piece and a small plain ferrule. The blade is straight and single-edged. It has a broad central fuller and bears traces of blue and gilt decoration over typical engraved designs which include the arms and cypher of the King. The blade is one of the many made in Germany and imported by J. J. Runkel from Solingen. The scabbard is of black leather with the usual three gilt brass mounts†. An interesting feature is the provision of D-shaped buckles instead of rings. These seem to have been employed on many swords during the period 1805–10 after which they virtually disappeared to be replaced by the more common circular pattern. The sword-knot attached is similar to that shown in Pellegrini's picture and is of the blue and gold cord variety with a fair-sized tassel at its end.

Blade: 32·5″   Hilt: 6″   N.M.M. 275

* Public Record Office, Adm. 3/154. The sword was probably ordered slightly earlier though the order itself has not been found.
† The top locket is engraved with the arms of Lord St. Vincent, bearing the escutcheon of pretence of the Strong family to which his wife belonged.

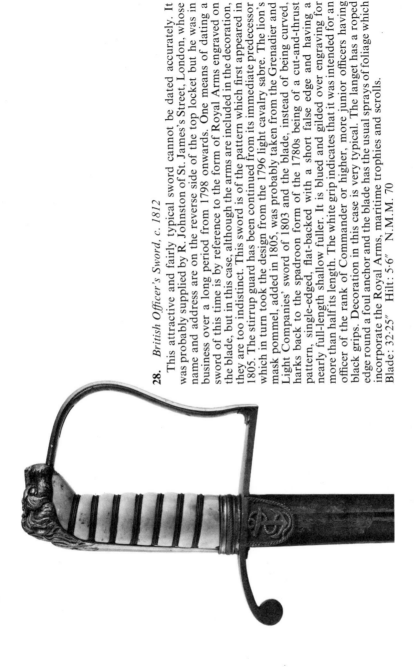

28. *British Officer's Sword, c. 1812*

This attractive and fairly typical sword cannot be dated accurately. It was probably supplied by R. Johnston of St. James's Street, London, whose name and address are on the reverse side of the top locket but he was in business over a long period from 1798 onwards. One means of dating a sword of this time is by reference to the form of Royal Arms engraved on the blade, but in this case, although the arms are included in the decoration, they are too indistinct. This sword is of the pattern which first appeared in 1805. The stirrup guard has been continued from its immediate predecessor which in turn took the design from the 1796 light cavalry sabre. The lion's mask pommel, added in 1805, was probably taken from the Grenadier and Light Companies' sword of 1803 and the blade, instead of being curved, harks back to the spadroon form of the 1780s being of a cut-and-thrust pattern, single-edged, flat-backed with a short false edge and having a nearly full-length shallow fuller. It is blued and gilded over engraving for more than half its length. The white grip indicates that it was intended for an officer of the rank of Commander or higher, more junior officers having black grips. Decoration in this case is very typical. The langet has a roped edge round a foul anchor and the blade has the usual sprays of foliage which incorporate the Royal Arms, maritime trophies and scrolls.

Blade: 32·25″   Hilt: 5·6″   N.M.M. 70

29, 30. *United States Fighting Sword, c. 1812*

This sword is firmly within the light cavalry tradition which was so marked in contemporary naval swords of both Britain and France. As if to emphasize that, it bears features of both British and French origin and is a particularly useful weapon from our point of view. Though not obviously a naval sword as such, it has a tradition of having formerly belonged to a naval officer and in both Britain and America swords originally intended for army officers were often employed at sea. The mixture of styles revealed by the hilt is worthy of considerable attention. The guard, which incorporates an obverse side-ring, is of the well-established straight stirrup form. A large additional branch or bar has been added to the obverse side which sweeps back horizontally before curving back on itself by way of the furthest extremity of the side-ring. It then divides into a foliated extension, which completes what is virtually a circle, and a scrolled continuation linking it with the stirrup. Within the circle is an oval plate supported by the letters U.S.A. This plate once contained a decorative device (the two rivet holes to which it was secured may still be seen) but unfortunately this is now missing; what it was is impossible to say but it seems likely that a national device, a displayed eagle perhaps, would be most likely in view of the lettering. The pommel is in the form of an eagle's head and is apparently the work of an established maker. Very similar castings are known on other swords and these seem to indicate that there must have been sufficient demand for this particular style spread over a period of years. An 1821 pattern United States Infantry officer's sword in the National Maritime Museum has a very similar pommel. The grip is of blackened wood, horizontally grooved and bound with twisted wire. The mounts are all of gilt brass. The blade is curved and flat-backed. It has a broad, shallow fuller running from an abbreviated shoulder for most of its length. It also has a short false edge. The decoration of the blade is engraved, blued and gilded. Most of this consists of foliate designs but these incorporate patriotic symbols in a way which was becoming increasingly common in the early nineteenth century. It is almost certain that this blade is German though its decoration could be either British or American. The style of decoration is British. The hilt, similarly, could be the work of a manufacturer in either country. The black leather scabbard has the usual three gilt brass mounts. The two lockets each have a ring for suspension and the chape is square tipped and is not provided with a shoe. This last feature was unlikely to commend itself to an army officer at this date even though the sword is just short enough to be worn suspended clear of the ground. The scabbard mounts are plain save for notched edges, a feature known but not very common in Britain.

Blade: 30"   Hilt: 5·3"   Captain G. B. K. Griffiths, R.M.(Ret.)

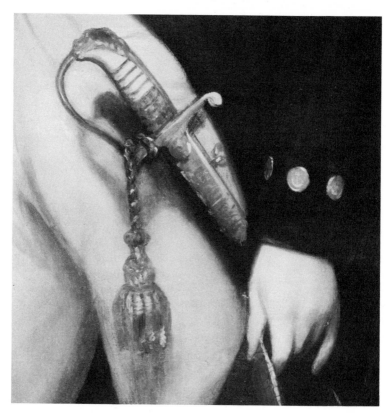

31. *Detail of a portrait of Edward Berry, 1815*

This portrait of Sir Edward Berry (1768–1831) was painted by John Singleton Copley in 1815. The subject, who is shown wearing the undress uniform of a Captain of over three years' seniority, had a particularly active and distinguished career which owed much to the interest taken in him by Lord Nelson. Berry's name became associated very much with one of Nelson's ships, H.M.S. *Agamemnon*, 64, in which they both served and which he commanded at Trafalgar in 1805. The sword introduced for officers of the rank of Commander and above in the same year as that battle is clearly shown by Copley in this picture. The stirrup guard, white (ivory) grip bound with gilt wire, single quillon, langets and lion's mask pommel are all fully apparent. The scabbard is of black leather and it has the then fashionable long top locket. Of particular interest is the sword-knot. It is of blue and gold cord, not tape, to the end of which is attached a large barrel with pendant bullions. It is very similar to those knots which appeared with swords awarded by the Patriotic Fund and, indeed, Berry received one of these swords for his services at Trafalgar.

N.M.M. G.H. 108

32. *Portrait of Edward Hawke, 1768/70*

Lord Hawke was born in 1705 and died in 1781. After a number of successful operations, he became famous for his action in Quiberon Bay in 1759 which put an end to French thoughts of invading Britain and prevented any reinforcement of the French in North America, a service which was to have the most profound effect on the future of the Thirteen Colonies. He is portrayed here in the general purpose uniform of a flag-officer of the period 1767–83. The painting is by Francis Cotes and was done between 1768 and 1770. It may be seen that, like many officers of his time, he wears a small-sword. This weapon is almost certainly silver-hilted and it has a knuckle-bow incorporating two quillons, a wire-bound grip and a single oval shell which has a decorative outline and is apparently covered with chased or chiselled designs. A sword-knot of blue and gold tape has been attached near the pommel and wound round the knuckle-bow before being taken under the rear quillon and brought forward to a knot. From this knot, its two ends appear and they are terminated by turk's heads from which stem gold and blue tassels. This painting shows not only a fairly typical small-sword, such as was worn on occasion for much of the eighteenth century, but also a quite usual way of attaching a sword-knot. It is fully apparent that any attempt to use the knot as a retaining strap would involve the owner in a fair amount of work. On the other hand, the presence of the blue and gold silk may mark this civilian sword as the property of a seaman. N.M.M. G.H. 30

33. *Portrait of John Paul Jones, 1779*

This engraving by R. Brookshaw shows Commodore Jones (1747–92) in the first uniform adopted by the Continental Navy of the United States. He wears what is obviously a small-sword which has a globular pommel, plain knuckle-guard and single oval shell. An interesting feature about this weapon, however, is its decoration which is in the form of a sword-knot of the tape variety. From what little detail that can be distinguished from the original engraving it appears that the tape itself is decorated with longitudinal stripes and terminates in a flat tassel. N.M.M.

34,35(Overleaf). *Small-Sword, c. 1780*

As small-swords took so great a variety of form there is probably little real purpose in devoting much space to them here. (The writings of Aylward and Peterson mentioned in the Bibliography offer a wider scope.) However, just as some of these essentially civilian swords were given service attributes by the addition of a blue and gold sword-knot, so others drew theirs from their decoration. A number of small-swords are known which bear engraved devices strongly indicative of the original owner's martial calling. The example shown here is one of these. The hilt is of gilt brass and the grip of wood covered by wire binding. An engraved Naval Crown surrounded by a laurel wreath is found on the pommel and on the ricasso and the shell bears engraved anchors, flags and pikes. The emphasis of the decoration, therefore, is naval and not simply of the more usual vague military form. The popularity of the colichemarde type of blade, one which narrows suddenly rather less than a quarter of its way from the hilt and then tapers evenly to the point, with service officers is another relevant point: the blade of this sword is of the usual colichemarde form. The scabbard is of black leather fitted with three gilt brass mounts, the top one bearing the engraved name and address of the cutler—Cullum, Charing Cross.

Blade: 31·4″ Hilt: 6·4″ N.M.M. 56

53

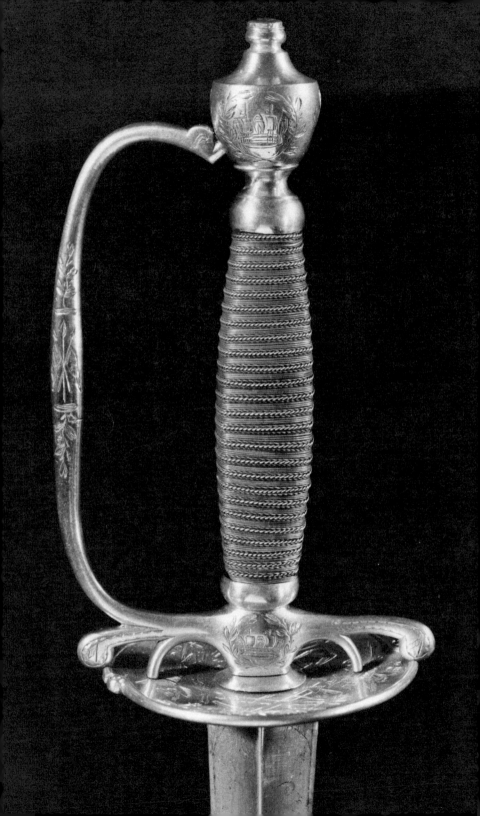

36. *British Presentation Sword, 1797*

Mention was made in the introduction of the practice of the City of London of making presentations in the small-sword style, even though that style was fast declining in popularity, at the end of the eighteenth century and at the beginning of the nineteenth. This sword is an example of that practice and a fairly early one at that. It was given to Admiral Viscount Duncan in commemoration of and as a reward for his victory over the Dutch fleet at Camperdown. The hilt is of silver-gilt set with pieces of translucent deep blue enamel and with polychrome enamel plaques. This particular photograph shows the hilt 'exploded' to demonstrate its construction and make the decoration rather clearer. The pommel bears the arms of Viscount Duncan (and those of the City of London on the reverse), a view of Duncan's flagship, H.M.S. *Venerable*, 74, is shown on the grip (with another view of the same ship on the reverse face) and the shell bears two pictures of the action within wreaths of laurel and oak. The blade is straight, of hollow triangular section and of even taper; it bears very little decoration. The scabbard is of blackened shagreen fitted with gilt mounts. Very similar swords were given to other senior officers who distinguished themselves in the war with Napoleon. Jervis, for example, received one for the Battle of St. Vincent and Nelson for the Nile. This hilt, like others for the same customer, was made by James Morrisset and the making up was by J. Makepeace. Later on, similar work was done by John Ray and James Montague and the making up by Rundle and Bridge.

Blade: 32·75"   Hilt: 7"   N.M.M. 91.0

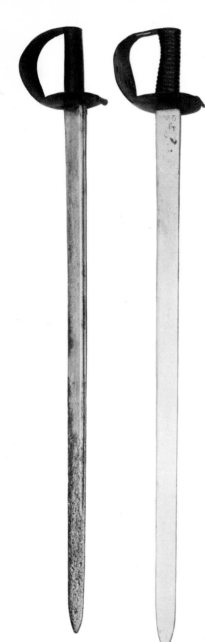

37. *Two British Cutlasses of the late 18th and early 19th centuries*

This illustration offers a useful means of comparing the tubular-gripped cutlass used in the 1790s with its replacement of 1804. The differences are fully apparent. The original design *(left)* is lighter and slightly smaller than that which replaced it. The double-disc form of the guard is less well developed and the blade is lighter and has a fuller next to the back edge. The 1804 cutlass *(right)*, on the other hand, has a grip shaped to the hand, a rather larger hilt and a slightly longer, heavier blade which is entirely flat. It will be noticed elsewhere that a later suggestion for an improved cutlass, in 1814 or thereabouts, involved a yet bigger hilt, though shortening the blade slightly and giving it a curve. There is, therefore, evidence of a more or less continuous desire on the part of some designers to improve what may not have been the most satisfactory of weapons. It may be seen, incidentally, that both cutlasses shown here have the rear edge of their respective stools rolled round upon themselves. It is probable that this was done to prevent snagging but it may also have strengthened the back of the guard. This feature disappeared for a while later in the nineteenth century and reappeared, probably as a result of a cavalry example, on the inner or reverse edge of the guard where clothing would be affected when the weapon was being worn. To what extent cutlasses were worn, as opposed to used, it is hard to say. Little is known about scabbards though it may be assumed that leather was employed fitted with metal, probably brass, mounts and that a frog stud was provided. Cutlasses were issued to ships, not seamen, so it is likely that they were not often worn during the period with which we are concerned. Almost certainly American practice was the same as this.

N.M.M. 411 and 350

38, 39. *British Cutlass, late 18th century*

This cutlass is probably an example of the first regulation cutlass ordered for the Royal Navy. This implication of uniformity, however, ought not to be taken too far. A number of manufacturers took part, through a series of contracts, in the supply of these weapons and it is far from certain that all their products looked alike. There are no marks on this weapon to indicate its origin but it bears a remarkable similarity to a sketch in the notebook kept by the artist Daniel Orme in his preliminary work for his painting of the Battle of Camperdown in 1798. Very similar weapons appeared in the United States; Mr. Peterson, in *The American Sword*, shows two examples (Nos. 46 and 47) and suggests that the two-disc type of hilt was in use in both countries as early as the late 1770s. British examples which may be positively dated earlier than about 1790 are, to the best of the author's knowledge, unknown so there is an outside chance that, far from America adopting a British style, Britain may have adopted an American. There is no evidence for this but it is far from being impossible. This cutlass has a wooden grip covered by a sheet of iron rolled round it and roughly welded. The resultant seam shows clearly in the photograph. The iron guard is an early example of the two-disc design which became so widespread with the second pattern British cutlass in 1804. The disc which protects the knuckles is rather less developed than that found rather later. The guard is secured to the pommel by the burred tip of the tang of the blade. The stool at the back of the guard is rolled upon itself, probably as a protection against snagging with clothing. The blade is straight, single-edged and has a flat back with a short false edge. A narrow fuller runs against the back from the hilt until the start of the false edge. It is interesting to speculate where this design of blade originated. It seems entirely possible that the British infantry hanger of the middle of the eighteenth century, a weapon which was withdrawn from service in 1768, may have provided the pattern. It is true that the majority of these hangers had slightly curved blades but there must have been many of these surplus articles in store after 1768 and many of these would have a blade which bore a narrow fuller near the back edge. The Board of Ordnance would not have shrunk from straightening blades if money could thereby be saved, so this might have happened here. The pattern of 1804 which replaced this one had uniformly flat (i.e., unfullered) blades. A further point which needs to be made is that formal Government inspection of swords which were purchased for the public service began in about 1800. The mark used was that of a crown over a figure or a crown on its own. These were stamped on the shoulders of each blade; although small, many can still be read quite clearly. The absence of such a mark, therefore, on a blade which is still in good condition, should indicate that it was made in the eighteenth century rather than the nineteenth. Some examples of the 1804 pattern are met which have a rounded tip to their blades instead of a point. It is probable that these are drill cutlasses, blunted some time after manufacture.

Blade: 28·5″ Hilt: 4·3″ N.M.M. 411

40, 41. *British or American Cutlass, c. 1814*

There is some evidence, in the proceedings of the Board of Ordnance in 1814, to suggest that the cutlass of the pattern introduced in 1804 was not proving suitable and that a new pattern was required. The Board corresponded with the firm of Tatham and Egg and from this exchange it is apparent that these makers designed a new type of cutlass hilt incorporating a new guard. Additional mention was made of one specimen which was to have a Tatham and Egg guard with an amended blade on the lines of one supplied by the Board with its end curved in a particular way. Several other patterns were mentioned but, thanks presumably to the peace which followed a year later, new patterns did not go into production and no issues of new cutlasses were made to the Royal Navy until the 1840s. All we can say, therefore, is that there was a flurry of activity in cutlass matters shortly before the end of the war with France in 1815. It is quite possible that the weapon illustrated here is a product of this activity. There is no means of telling who made it or when, but as the Royal Navy purchased no new cutlasses from 1816 to 1841 it is highly probable, in view of the design of the hilt, that this example was made before that period. Although the guard and the grip are both very similar to those found on 1804 cutlasses they are both larger than normal. Minor variations can be accepted, of course, in the ordinary way as following on from the practice of placing contracts for supply with a number of different manufacturers and it is unlikely that the Board was over concerned with such details as particularly accurate measurements since blade lengths can vary by nearly an inch. But this example lies outside even these tolerances. The disc designed to protect the knuckles is longer and wider than that normally found on 1804 pattern cutlasses and is more pear-than disc-shaped. The horizontal disc is also larger and the strip of iron connecting the two is consequently shorter, though wider, than before. The cast iron grip is not much changed apart from being longer. It is still horizontally grooved and retains the few vertical cuts of the 1804 pattern. The blade, however, is entirely different. It is rather shorter than before and is wider and, above all, slightly curved. Still flat-backed, it bears a narrow fuller near the back edge which may owe something to the French *Montmorencie* style. Most interestingly, it is slightly falchion-shaped, perhaps as a result of the success of the 1796 light cavalry blade. There is no scabbard and it is quite possible that none was ever designed. It may be seen that there is some evidence to suggest that this weapon was a British prototype which never went into production. But rather similar weapons have appeared in the United States, in Baltimore, and Mr. Peterson describes one of these in *The American Sword* (No. 48). Although not the same as this one, the Baltimore cutlass is similar enough to raise the question of this example's nationality. Variations in style and dimension occurred in the United States for the same reason—a multiplicity of suppliers—as in Britain. The present whereabouts of any weapon are not, *per se*, of any relevance when trying to determine its origin but there is a clear possibility that this cutlass illustrated here is American rather than British. The absence of marks, which may simply be due to the damaged condition of the blade, prevents us from finding an answer to this question and only further evidence in the shape of either written sources or further examples with marks will help.

Blade: 26·5″ Hilt: 5″   N.M.M. 409

42. *British Hanger cum Cutlass, c. 1805*

Although, in both Britain and the United States, regulation patterns of cutlass appeared towards the end of the eighteenth century, unofficial types continued in service. These types probably disappeared from the two navies fairly quickly but must have remained common in merchant vessels for quite some time. The example illustrated here is of interest for a number of reasons. The grip, obviously, is very like that found on British naval cutlasses from 1804 and was presumably made originally for such a weapon: it is of cast iron with both horizontal and vertical grooving. The brass guard is of the stirrup pattern and too long. It is plain save for the incised letters W I D C No 11. Almost certainly these initials stand for West India Dock Company and thus this weapon is one of those issued to the Company's police force, a body established to protect ships from the depredations of thieves in the River Thames and the ancestors of the modern Thames Division of the Metropolitan Police. The blade is a curiosity and may, conceivably, be modelled on that of the British cavalry sabre of 1788. It is curved, single-edged and flat-backed and has a narrow fuller against the back edge running for about three-quarters of the total length. The royal cypher GR on the blade is of a form which became more common in the nineteenth century and which is rather more compact than that used previously. Any scabbard that was issued with this weapon is now missing. The associated nature of this weapon is clear but it in no way detracts from its interest.

Blade: 24·75″   Hilt: 4·5″   Mr. R. L. Kelly

43. *Portrait of George Darby, 1783*

George Darby (*c.* 1720–90) does not seem to have been the most energetic of naval officers. His career was largely uneventful save for the second relief of Gibraltar in 1781 which he led. This portrait was begun two years later; the artist, George Romney, apparently began it in 1783 but seems to have finished it later. Darby is shown in the uniform of a flag-officer of the period 1774–83, but his buttons are grouped in threes as was ordered for Vice-Admirals in the period 1783–7. What is of the greatest interest, however, is that he is portrayed wearing a dirk. As the guard of this weapon is apparently formed of a cross-piece with inversed finials and as the length of blade is insufficient to clear the line of his hat, let alone his coat, it must be very short. This is probably the earliest properly observed pictorial evidence available which demonstrates the wearing of a dirk and it is strange that a flag-officer should be wearing it. The grip is dark brown in colour and bound with wire and the hilt mounts are yellow—and presumably, therefore, of brass—as is the top locket of the brown scabbard. The dirk is worn from a sling or slings attached to a waistbelt worn under the waistcoat. Although earlier dirks are known, this particular picture furnishes an early piece of independent evidence, which is exceptionally scarce.
N.M.M.

44. *Dirk, late 18th century*

This dirk is included here as an example of the use to which damaged swords and their blades were occasionally put. This weapon was probably originally a broadsword, the blade of which was broken and repointed. A new hilt was provided but the existing scabbard seems to have been shortened to fit the altered blade. The bone grip is bound spirally with silver ribbon. The hilt mounts are, unusually, of iron and consist of a pommel cap and short cross-guard with inversed finials. In the short fuller of the blade is incised the name SAHA-ǴUM. The scabbard has iron mounts but these do not include a chape, the end of the leather being simply sewn. Although this dirk is in damaged condition it exhibits a number of points of interest. The 'signature' is probably a German attempt to forge that of the Toledo family of Sahagun— this sort of practice was widespread in Europe in the eighteenth century. The owner of this weapon is thought to have been John Samuel Smith who was commissioned Lieutenant in the Royal Navy in 1806, was court-martialled the following year and sentenced to remain at the bottom of the list of Lieutenants for six years, was reinstated in 1813 but was still a Lieutenant when he died in 1840. The practice of making a new weapon out of a broken sword must be very long established but it is unlikely that it is the origin of the dirk as such.

Blade: 12·6"   Hilt: 4·5"
N.M.M. 271

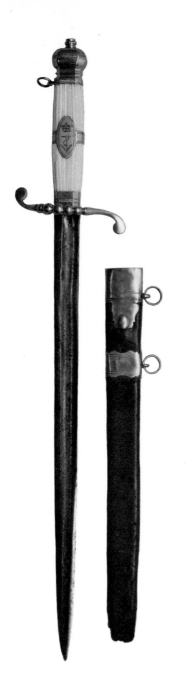

45. *British Bead-Hilted Dirk, c. 1790*

Although the practice of wearing companion daggers with swords had virtually disappeared in western Europe and America by the end of the eighteenth century, some regard was still had to this long-established fashion. There is some suggestion that it was more popular in the United States than in Britain for a man to possess both a sword and a dirk which reflected some of its features. This slight continuing tradition is well illustrated by this dirk which bears a family resemblance to the type of sword shown in Plate 19. The grip of this weapon is also of vertically reeded ivory and the gilt brass cushion pommel is also very similar to that of the sword.* The only real difference lies in the dirk's abbreviated guard yet this bears a side-ring decorated with five beads. The blade, like that of the sword, is single-edged and flat-backed with a small false edge and a broad shallow fuller. It is, in shortened form, a version of the cut-and-thrust blade found on the sword. The black leather scabbard has two gilt lockets, each with a ring, and once had a gilt chape. The decoration of the mounts, as usual at this time, is restricted to groups of engraved threads. This dirk scabbard is very similar, apart from its length, to the scabbards most often associated with bead-hilted spadroons in the Royal Navy.

Blade: 14·75″   Hilt: 5·5″   N.M.M.7

* The provision of a ring at the pommel indicates that a dirk-knot could be fitted and represents a fairly early example of such a practice with dirks.

46. *British Naval Dirk, c. 1798*

This attractive little weapon has, at first sight, nothing about it to connect it with the sea; but aspects of its decoration put it into a military context of some form and its similarity to other weapons known to have belonged to naval officers makes it worthy of inclusion here. It is somewhat more ornate than most other eighteenth-century dirks and probably represents a transitional form between the largely plain, workaday weapons of the last quarter of the century and the more ornate examples of the first quarter of the following one. The hilt is of turned and polished ivory decorated with vertical flutes. The pommel is entirely of ivory, a feature which is far less common than those fitted with a metal cap. Hilt mounts are of gilt brass decorated with embossed foliage and scrolls and the guard is straight with acorn finials. This last feature was to reappear in British dirk design and only disappear when the dirk itself went into abeyance in 1939. The blade is straight, double-edged and of flattened diamond section. It is lightly engraved with military music devices (trumpet and drums) and foliage and was once blued and gilt. The black leather scabbard has the usual three gilt brass mounts decorated in a conventional way. The dual means of suspension probably indicates a change in the fashion of wearing such a weapon.
Blade: 12·4″ Hilt: 3·5″ N.M.M. 217

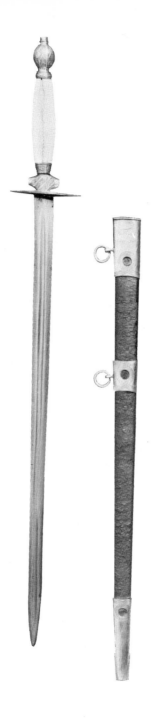

47. *British Dirk, 1800*

This dirk is an example of a type known to exist in fair numbers, most of them British and most having had their quillons removed. An occasional example is met which retains its quillons and these extend beyond the line of the small oval shell and are relatively straight and plain though often have vertically recurved finials. The grip is of white ivory, cross-hatched overall and all mounts are of gilt brass engraved with diagonal strapwork and foliage. The blade is straight with a narrow central fuller and is double-edged. The black leather scabbard bears the usual three gilt mounts. This particular example bears the name of a London cutler—TATHAM, ADMIRALTY—in a form which indicates that it dates from the period 1800–2. It is very unlikely that the design is Tatham's own and as there are so many still in existence it is interesting to speculate what their origin might be. There is nothing about this weapon to indicate a connection with the sea, but the same is true of most eighteenth-century dirks. As few army officers, British or American, seem to have worn dirks to any great extent and as large numbers of naval officers did there is a strong presumption that these belonged to the latter. The whole group of weapons similar to this one furnishes yet another example of the influence of fashion on the design of personal arms.
Blade: 16·25″   Hilt: 5·4″   N.M.M. 59

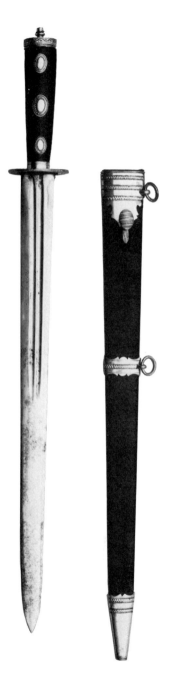

48. *'Dirk', c. 1800*

There is nothing maritime about this weapon although it is attributed to Admiral Sir William Cornwallis. It is included here, however, because it demonstrates a number of important and continuing influences found in Britain and America. The design is probably German in origin and intended originally for use by a huntsman. The presence of three devices on the grip reflects a common European (especially German and French) form favoured for hunting weapons. These are occasionally met with on British and American dirks; this example is a case in point and the dirk of Captain John Downes in the U.S. Naval Academy Museum is another. Some three decades at least separate these two weapons, but this shows that hunting styles were still followed to some extent at sea at the end of our period and even after having already served for the best part of two centuries. This particular weapon has a wooden grip with gilt brass mounts which include a small circular guard. The blade is straight and double-edged with two small fullers each side. It is possibly somewhat older than the hilt. The black leather scabbard has gilt brass mounts, the top one of which bears the name of a Portsmouth cutler, William Read.

Blade: 16"   Hilt: 5"   N.M.M. 202

49. *British Curved Dirk, 1801–24*

The curved dirk seems to have become popular in the United States rather earlier than in Britain. The style appeared in the United States round about 1800 or very shortly after, whereas it is unlikely that it was known in Britain before about 1805. There is even the suggestion that it did not appear in Britain until after the raid on Copenhagen in 1807 and then in emulation of Danish patterns. But the concept of a curved dirk blade was common in France and it is probably from that country that both Britain and America took the style. These weapons can often only be dated by reference to general artistic considerations, but the example shown here bears on the top locket of the scabbard the name J. Salter and the address at which he worked from 1801 to 1824. The blade bears the stamped letter G on the obverse side immediately next to the guard and this may stand for the Birmingham family of Gill who were in business from 1774 to 1826. It can be seen, therefore, that this weapon dates from the very end of our period and may, conceivably, have been made even later. Yet many features of its design are similar to those found in Britain in the first decade of the nineteenth century. The ivory grip is shaped to the hand and cross-hatched. The hilt mounts are of gilt brass and include a lion's mask pommel which bears a small loop to which there may once have been attached a ring to take a dirk-knot, and a simple guard with small side-rings. The blade is of flattened oval section, being double-edged —a relatively uncommon feature. The black leather scabbard, unlike the rest of the weapon, bears the obvious maritime motif of a foul anchor as well as an engraved, and fairly conventional, military trophy.
Blade: 16·6″   Hilt: 4·4″   N.M.M. 20

50. *British Naval Dirk, c. 1810*

This ornate little weapon demonstrates the growing feeling in favour of highly decorated pieces which roughly coincides with the period of the Regency in Britain. In comparison with its eighteenth-century forebears it is particularly highly decorated. The grip is of yellowed ivory and the mounts of gilt brass. The fairly common device (by this time) of a lion's head at the pommel has been replaced by the recumbent figure of a complete lion and this is found on some swords as well in the first quarter of the nineteenth century. A chain knuckle-guard was once fitted between the finial of the leading quillon and the pommel and the small rings for its retention may still be seen. The langets are more decorative than usual. The blade is curved and flat-backed. Once decorated with engraving (which unusually includes the Crown over GR device) as well as being blued and gilt, the blade must originally have set off the hilt extremely well. Unhappily, it has been extensively damaged. The scabbard is of black leather and has three ornate mounts. The engraving of these fittings includes the widespread use of an acanthus motif and, on the chape, a lion's mask.

Blade: 13·1″   Hilt: 5″   N.M.M. 247

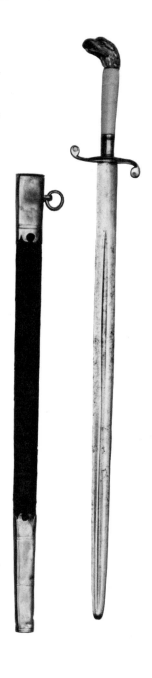

51. *American Dirk, c. 1815*

As was noted above, the dirk as a weapon had as chequered a career in the United States as it did in Britain, but in both countries naval officers wore them and in time they came to be regarded as the badge of midshipmen though the reason for this is unclear. This attractive little weapon has a finely cast and chased gilt brass eagle's head pommel. The grip is of turned ivory and gently shaped being widest near the pommel. Its other end is secured by a relatively deep ferrule decorated with engraved threads. The cross-guard has a small side-ring and disc finials. The fore quillon is pierced, as is the eagle's beak, to take a chain knuckle-guard which, unhappily, is now missing. The blade is straight, double-edged and of flattened oval section. It has a narrow fuller running centrally for most of its length each side. The point, which is rounded, has apparently been damaged at some time. The black leather scabbard has a gilt brass top locket, fitted with a ring, and a gilt brass chape with a squared tip. There is no sign that any other means of suspension was ever fitted which makes this single ring suspension rather unusual in British and American terms. There are no marks to indicate the origins of this weapon but the nature of the eagle's head suggests very strongly that it is appropriate to the United States though where it was made it is impossible to say.

Blade: 13·4″   Hilt: 4″   N.M.M. 385

52. *British Presentation Sword, 1798*

After the Battle of the Nile, on 1 August 1798, the captains of the victorious fleet established the Egyptian Club in commemoration of the action. They also presented to the fleet commander, Horatio Nelson, a sword as a token of their admiration. It seems that subsequently a number of members of the Egyptian Club had swords made for themselves in imitation of that which they had given to Nelson and this weapon is probably an example of one of those imitations. It is likely that the model on which this was based had a gold hilt whereas this has one of gilt brass. At least one other sword is known which has a very similar hilt and others have been mentioned in the past. The grip is cast and chased in the form of a crocodile and bears on its obverse side a polychrome enamel picture of the battle. A plaque of similar size on the reverse reads 'VICTORY OF THE NILE, 1ST OF AUGUST 1798'. The knuckle-bow form of guard broadens to incorporate an oval shield and then a leaf-shaped stool with beaded edge. The straight blade is double-edged and of flattened diamond section and bears the engraved legend 'FOR MY COUNTRY AND KING' on a narrow flat formed on the central rib. The scabbard is of black leather fitted with two gilt lockets and a gilt chape. The blade is presumably German but the sword was made up by the well-known firm of jewellers Rundell and Bridge who were concerned with a number of presentation swords. As this sword was probably made to personal order it is technically incorrect to describe it as a presentation piece; but it is so described because it was based on a weapon which was indeed a present.
Blade: 31″   Hilt: 7″   N.M.M. 94

53. *Hilt of Presentation Sword of the Patriotic Fund at Lloyd's, 1804*

The official description of this hilt, and the reasons for the motifs chosen, is as follows:

The ornamental design for the hilts of the swords Presented from this Fund, in reward of British Valour, imports that National Union (figured by the Roman Fasces) produces Herculean Efforts (of which the club of Hercules is emblematic) which, aided by Wisdom (denoted by the Serpent) Lead to Victory (implied by the skin of the Nemean Lion, the proudest of that Hero's Trophies) The Wreath of Laurel denotes that Rewards await the Brave who shall successfully wield their Swords in the Cause of their Country, in Defence of British Security, Independence and Honour.

It must be rare for so full an account to be given of the reasons implied by the design of a sword-hilt. The normal practice seems to have been to let various conventional emblems speak for themselves. The quillon block, not mentioned in the official description, bears an embossed trophy of flags, rudder, gun, pile of shot and anchor. The work is carried out entirely in gilt brass save for the grip which is of ivory cross-hatched for roughly three-quarters of its total surface. Although blades and scabbards varied in accordance with value, hilts were more or less uniform in design and any variations are unimportant. It can be seen that the stirrup form was used, albeit in angular form opposite the pommel, allied to a lion's mask. This may have had some influence on the sword adopted by the Royal Navy in 1805. The blade of the Patriotic Fund sword owes its shape to the British Light Cavalry sword of 1796 being curved and slightly falchion-shaped. Most of these swords were set up by one cutler, Teed of Lancaster Court, but at least one sword is known which was produced by Salter.
N.M.M. 389

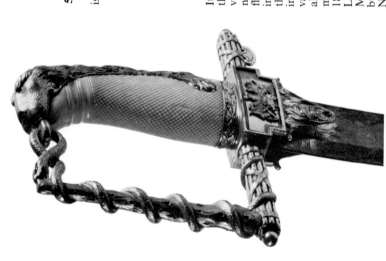

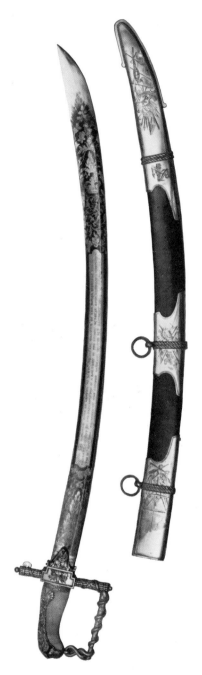

54. *Presentation Sword from the Patriotic Fund at Lloyd's, 1804*

This ornate weapon is an example of the £30 grade of sword presented by the Patriotic Fund at Lloyd's. It was presented to Lieutenant William Walker, Royal Marines, for his services at Martinique in November 1803. Although superficially very different, it can be seen that its design owes much to the Light Cavalry form adopted by the British Army in 1796 and by the Navy a few years later. The ivory grip is shaped to the hand, the guard is a variation of the stirrup form, langets are fitted and the blade is of the slight falchion shape which was so popular. The gilt brass hilt is of a form common to all Patriotic Fund swords but the blade's decoration is distinctive and quite unlike that of the £50 and £100 swords. This decoration consists of gilt floral sprays on a blued ground, an all-gilt dull and bright panel containing the circumstances of the award and further foliate forms incorporating the Royal Cypher and the crown. The blueing itself terminates in a foliated form leaving the tip of the blade bright polished steel. The reverse side of the blade is similar but includes a representation of Britannia, the Royal Arms and a spray of the national flower emblems. The scabbard is of black morocco leather fitted with engraved gilt brass mounts. The suspension rings are secured by simulated bands of rope, a feature which was to become quite common on naval swords in both Britain and America in the nineteenth century. The engraved designs contain a mixture of classical and maritime motifs typical of this period.
Blade: 29·9″ Hilt: 6·5″ N.M.M. 389

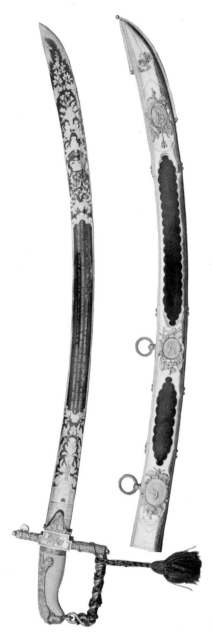

55. *Presentation Sword from the Patriotic Fund at Lloyd's, 1804*

The family connection between this sword and the preceding illustration is obvious. The only differences lie in the decoration of the blade and in the design of the scabbard. This is an example of the £50 type, the most common awarded by the Patriotic Fund. It was presented to Captain Henry Wilson who commanded the East India Company's ship *Warley*. This vessel, primarily a trading ship but carrying the gun armament of a frigate, formed part of a Company's convoy under the command of Commodore Nathaniel Dance. The convoy was attacked by a French squadron under Rear-Admiral Linois, with his flag in the *Marengo*, 80, in the Malacca Strait in February 1804, having sailed from Canton shortly before. By handling his fleet with consummate skill, Dance drove off and then pursued the enemy and both he and his captains were rewarded when they reached London. The scabbard is essentially of black leather encased in gilt brass so that only two panels of leather actually show on each side. Its decoration is in relief whereas that of the £30 sword is engraved. As was very common at this time, the decorative motifs have classical origins largely concerned with the labours of Hercules. The blade is almost entirely blued and gilt and bears a brief description of the circumstances of the award on its obverse side. The remainder of the decoration consists of gilt foliage and scrolls together with a representation of the Royal Cypher all on a blued ground. The decoration of the reverse is similar but includes the Royal Arms and the goddess Victory with some of her attributes.

Blade: 30·1″   Hilt: 6·5″   N.M.M. 42

56. *Scabbard of the Trafalgar Pattern of the Patriotic Fund at Lloyd's, 1805*

The third and fourth groups of swords awarded by the Patriotic Fund were very similar to each other and took most of their style from the two cheaper varieties. Blades were very like those found on £50 swords and hilts were virtually identical, but scabbards differed markedly. The covering of the wooden lining was of black or dark blue velvet. Like the £50 scabbard, this only showed in two slots on each side, but in the case of the £100 and Trafalgar patterns the velvet was overlaid, within the slots, with embossed and pierced decoration. Again, and not surprisingly, this took the form of classical devices arranged as trophies which incorporated specifically maritime emblems. In place of the two suspension rings normally found on swords of this period including the £30 and £50 presentation pieces, the £100 and Trafalgar patterns had serpents of gilt brass formed into a loop through which the spring clips at the ends of belt slings could pass. Differences between £100 and Trafalgar swords are relatively minor. The Trafalgar pattern was basically a £100 type of scabbard with some additional decoration relating to the battle itself. All swords awarded by the Fund were supplied with a mahogany box, which bore the trade card of the supplier inside the lid, and also enclosed an ornamental belt. These were of leather covered with blue velvet and decorated with woven gilt wire and sequins. The buckle was circular in shape and two slings were attached. It is not likely that any of these swords were ever worn much. Lord St. Vincent refused to allow them to be worn at all but, not unnaturally, a number of recipients are portrayed wearing them with full-dress uniforms at a later date. N.M.M. 171

57. *British Presentation Sword, 1810*

This sword shows, in a restrained way, how contemporary regulation patterns could be used as a basis for a presentation form yet still comply with the spirit of the regulations. The pattern of sword introduced in Britain in 1805 for Commanders and above, of which this is a rather ornate example, was a suitable vehicle for this practice. The hilt mounts of gilt brass are more or less as ordered but are more ornately decorated. The lion's mask pommel, with a short mane, is entirely typical but the decoration of the back-piece, in extension of that mane, is not. Similarly, the stirrup guard and langets are regulation in form but the decoration then applied serves to distinguish the weapon from its regulation counterparts. The blade is straight, single-edged and flat-backed. It is etched with a brief account of the circumstances of the presentation: Henry Duncan, Captain

of the *Mercury*, gave this sword to his 1st Lieutenant for the gallantry and leadership displayed in two boat actions in 1809. That Lieutenant, Watkin Owen Pell, also received a £50 sword from the Patriotic Fund at Lloyd's for the first of these actions. The scabbard is of black leather with the usual three gilt brass mounts. Instead of the restrained engraved thread decoration normally found on swords of this pattern, however, this scabbard has heavily embossed lockets and chape bearing the fairly common classical military allusions.

Blade: 28″   Hilt: 5″   N.M.M. 40

Select Bibliography

Although many works exist, in both Britain and America, which deal with aspects of the history of edged weapons, only a few are much concerned with those used at sea. Among those which are of interest in this context are the following.

Aylward, J. D., *The Small-Sword in England*, London, 1960

Blair, Claude, *European and American Arms*, London, 1962

Bosanquet, Captain H. T. A., *The Naval Officer's Sword*, London, 1955

ffoulkes, Charles, and Hopkinson, E. C., *Sword, Lance and Bayonet*, London, 1967

Jarrett, Dudley, *British Naval Dress*, London, 1960

May, W. E., and Annis, P. G. W., *Swords for Sea Service*, London, 1970

—— and Kennard, A. N., *Naval Swords and Firearms*, London, 1968

Neumann, G. C., *History of Weapons of the American Revolution*, New York, 1967

Norman, A. V. B., *Small-Swords and Military Swords*, London, 1967

Peterson, H. L., *Arms and Armor in Colonial America*, Harrisburg, 1956

—— *The American Sword*, Philadelphia, 1965 (This edition includes *American Silver Mounted Swords 1700–1815*, by the same author)

—— *Daggers and Fighting Knives of the Western World*, London and New York, 1968

—— 'U.S. Naval Dirks' in *The American Arms Collector*, No. 1, Vol. II, January 1958

Spinney, J. D., 'Types of Sword worn by British Sea Officers during the War of American Independence' in *Mariner's Mirror*, Vol. 50 (1964), pp. 135–6

Tily, Captain J. C., *The Uniforms of the United States Navy*, New York, 1964

Wilkinson, Frederick, *Swords and Daggers*, London and New York, 1968

The work published by the Company of Military Collectors and Historians, on both navies, is another fruitful source of information.

Principal Collections

A fair number of useful collections of naval edged weapons exist in both Britain and the United States. Large numbers of important weapons, on the other hand, are in private hands in both countries as well. Among the more important public collections are the following.

Britain
National Maritime Museum, Greenwich
The Armouries, H.M. Tower of London
The London Museum
The Victoria and Albert Museum
The Scottish United Services Museum, Edinburgh

United States of America
United States National Museum, Washington, D.C.
Metropolitan Museum, New York, N.Y.
United States Naval Academy Museum, Annapolis, Md.
Also a number of museums controlled by the National Parks Service, Department of the Interior, and State and City historical society collections—particularly, but by no means exclusively, those situated within the boundaries of the Thirteen Colonies.

The Wearing of Swords

About the year 1660 seamen generally wore their hangers and their small-swords suspended by two relatively short slings from a waist-belt. Fashions of wearing these varied. Where a man is portrayed in armour of any description the belt is worn around the base of the breastplate; but as we have seen, it is very unlikely that armour was much worn at all. The long close-fastening coat of the late seventeenth and early eighteenth centuries presented rather more of a problem. In some portraits the waistbelt is shown being worn outside the coat, while in others it is entirely hidden and the sword itself protrudes through the heavy pleat on the left hip. This practice often led to the coat being badly bunched forward of the pleat which would seem to indicate that the relatively short slings then popular were used even when they were not strictly long enough because the sword needed to be suspended high up to prevent its being an encumbrance. Small-swords were worn from similar belts though, as the front of the coat might be left open, their hilts could project at the front as an alternative to the pleat. Civilian fashion would normally only countenance a hidden belt but seamen seem often to have preferred to wear their coats fastened and their belts on full view. It may be that this was a reflection of current military styles and was, therefore, an indication of the wearer's calling.

The slings of these waistbelts are of interest because the forward one appears to have been relatively long, being secured near or at the belt buckle. Later belts, as we shall see, tended to have long rear slings which would take most of the weight of the weapon on the forward one, this being attached some inches back from the buckle.

Little change seems to have taken place until the middle of the eighteenth century. In the 1740s, the metal hanger or clip which fitted into the waistband of the breeches appeared. This had two short chain slings and increasingly came into use with small-swords. The coats worn at this time were cut further back than formerly and the sword itself was suspended at an angle which permitted its hilt to protrude forward of the base of the lapel. The introduction of naval uniform in Britain in 1748 does not seem to have had any effect on this since all coats, especially those for full dress, were cut in the civilian style. The rather more military double-breasted un-dress coat occasionally bore an external belt but it was cut sufficiently high in front for the belt to be hidden either by the coat itself or by the long waistcoat and still to leave the sword free.

The relative increase in weight and dimensions of sidearms was probably partly responsible for a major change in the way in which they were worn. Army styles must also have had some effect. Small-swords and other relatively light weapons continued to be worn in the way outlined above but the larger military types began to appear, from about 1780, suspended in a frog attached to a leather belt worn over the right shoulder and resting on the left hip. The frog usually consisted of a tapered tube of leather sewn to the shoulder belt, into which the scabbard could be inserted. Often a hook or stud was attached to the top locket and this passed through a slot cut in the frog thus rendering it more secure. It appears that the shoulder belt appeared at sea at about the same time as boots of a military pattern first made their appearance there. The shoulder belt did not last very long so far as officers were concerned, declining in the early years of the nineteenth century. The return to a waistbelt followed, but this time, apart from a short period after the adoption of uniform styles of belt, unequal slings became the rule, the rear sling being longer (often much longer) than the other. The belts which accompanied the swords awarded by the Patriotic Fund were all of this pattern and the first regulation belts were the same.

Dirks were worn both in frogs and from short slings. Their light weight and small size made them manageable enough though it may be suggested that the larger examples are more commonly found with a frog stud on their lockets rather than rings.

Some swords and dirks are found to have scabbards equipped with both a stud and rings. This can indicate a change in the fashion of suspension, usually from the former to the latter, but there is often a more practical explanation. When a man was engaged in boat work or in any other activity where agility was required and a sidearm, though necessary, might prove cumbersome, additional means of securing that weapon might have been found necessary.

It is doubtful if any regulation method of suspension was ever applied to the cutlass. Shoulder belts with frogs were known as were waistbelts and simple lengths of rope worn round the waist. As cutlasses were rarely worn, as opposed to used, it is probable that ratings snatched them up when required. If these men were landed and had muskets as well as cutlasses then some means of wearing the latter would have been needed. Later cutlasses seem always to have been worn in frogs.